Exploring this Land from Coast to Coast to Coast

Vivien Bowers

Illustrated by Dan Hobbs and Dianne Eastman

MAPLE
TREE
PRESS

Maple Tree Press books are published by Owlkids Books Inc.
10 Lower Spadina Ave., Suite 400, Toronto, Ontario M5V 2Z2, www.owlkids.com

Text © 1999, 2007, 2009 Vivien Bowers   Illustrations © 1999, 2007, 2009 Dan Hobbs and Dianne Eastman

Distributed in Canada by Raincoast Books, 9050 Shaughnessy Street, Vancouver, British Columbia V6P 6E5
Distributed in the United States by Publishers Group West, 1700 Fourth Street, Berkeley, California 94710

Author's Dedication

To my real family, who shared the road across Canada with me: Eric, whose humour is a wonderful gift; Joel, without whom my life would be just plain dull; and Guy, whose unique perspective on the world inspired this book.

Acknowledgements

The author would like to thank the following individuals and companies for their help in various ways during the research and writing of this book: VIA Rail; Eddie and Irene Amagonalok and family; Sue and Bert Port and Linda Kennedy; Rob, Kyle, Rachel, Sean, and Frances Heisler; Sheba and Jerry Meland; Denise and David Kendall; Relais Nordik Inc.; Kim and Louise Poole; Heather Pengelley; Pauline Clift; Laura Jackson

Cataloguing in Publication Data

Bowers, Vivien, 1951-
 Wow, Canada! : exploring this land from coast to coast to coast / Vivien Bowers ; illustrated by Dan Hobbs and Dianne Eastman. -- Tenth anniversary ed.

Includes index.
ISBN 978-1-897349-82-3 (bound).--ISBN 978-1-897349-83-0 (pbk.)

 1. Canada--Juvenile literature. 2. Canada--Geography--Juvenile literature. 3. Canada--Description and travel--Juvenile literature. I. Hobbs, Dan II. Eastman, Dianne III. Title.

FC58.B685 2009   j917.1   C2009-905096-X

Library of Congress Control Number: 2009908532

Design & art direction: Dianne Eastman   *Electronic assembly:* Greg Hall   *Illustrations:* Dan Hobbs (colour), Dianne Eastman (black and white)

We acknowledge the financial support of the Canada Council for the Arts, the Ontario Arts Council, the Government of Canada through the Book Publishing Industry Development Program (BPIDP), and the Government of Ontario through the Ontario Media Development Corporation's Book Initiative for our publishing activities.

Canada Council   Conseil des Arts
for the Arts   du Canada

ONTARIO ARTS COUNCIL
CONSEIL DES ARTS DE L'ONTARIO

Photo credits
All photos by V. Bowers, except front cover (mountain), 8 (left/right), 9 (above/below), 11 (postcard), 12 (above/below), 13 (Chinatown/gondola/Skytrain/skyline), 14 (top left/bear), 14–15 (mountain): Tourism B. C.; 18: killer whale/©Parks Canada*/10.104.10.03(70); 22 (top, left): Canada Olympic Park; 22–23 (3 photos, bottom): Calgary Exhibition and Stampede; 24 (above/below): The Friends of Head-Smashed-In Buffalo Jump; 25: rattlesnake/PC/08.81.10.01(01); 28 (bottom): D. Eastman; 29 (bottom): West Edmonton Mall; 34 (antelope), 34–35 (geese), 35 (upper), 36 (prairie dog/grain elevator), 37 (lightning), 38 and 38–39 (RCMP), 39 (Snowbirds, above/below), 40 (postcard/2 slides, bottom), 41 (2 slides, bottom): Tourism Saskatchewan; 46 (The Forks): The Forks North Portage Partnership; 46 (bottom): The Royal Canadian Mint; 47 (bottom): Riel House/PC/F. Cattroll/H.07.71.01.04(01); 50–51 (5 slides, bottom): Folklorama/A. Sikorsky; 51 (grass): Living Prairie Museum/C. Shea; 55 (top): Pukaskwa National Park/PC/F. Mayrs/06.63.03.18(10); 55 (middle): Pukaskwa N. P./PC/M. Beedell/06.63.03.20(25); 55 (bottom): Pukaskwa N. P./PC/Barrett & Mackay/06.63.03.20(105); 56 (left): monarch butterflies/PC/J. R. Graham/06.62.10.02(54); 56–57: Bruce Peninsula/PC/V. Last/06.64.03.20(41); 66 (bottom, left): indigo bunting/PC/Graham/06.62.10.02(105); 66 (bottom, middle): scarlet tanager/PC/Graham/06.62.10.01(115); cape may warbler/PC/Graham/06.62.10.02(95); 74 (top, left): National Battlefields/PC/Cattroll/H.05.58.04.03(31); 74 (top, right): National Battlefields/PC/P. St-Jacques/H.05.58.04.03(05); 78 (top): Forillon N. P./PC/St-Jacques/05.50.03.13(35); 78 (middle): Forillon N. P./PC/St-Jacques/05.50.03.20(253); 79 (middle, left): northern gannet/PC/M. Finkelstein/01.10.10.02(13); 79 (middle, right): gannets/PC/Finkelstein/01.10.10.02(11); 79 (bottom): Forillon N. P./PC/St-Jacques/05.50.04.09(142); 86 (top): Province House/PC/J. Butterill/H.02.22.01.01(41); 86 (middle): Province House/PC/Butterill/H.02.22.06.09(09); 86 (bottom): Province House/PC/Cattroll/H.02.22.06.05(19); 88 (top): Prince Edward Island N. P./PC/D. Ford/02.20.03.20(17); 88 (right): P. E. I. N. P./PC/T. Grant/02.20.03.01(165); 92 (top, left), 98 (lower, left): Tourism New Brunswick/B. Atkinson; 92 (lower, left), 95 (postcard/fiddler), 96 (bottom), 97 (full page/inset), 99 (puffin/seals): Tourism N. B.; 93 (top): Tourism N. B./D. Madison; 94: Tourism N. B./G. Stott; 96 (upper/middle): Tourism N. B./A. Gallant; 99 (herring): Tourism N. B./S. Homer; 102 (top): Cape Breton Highlands N. P./PC/A. Cornellier/03.30.03.20(241); 103 (top): Grand Pré/PC/A. Guindon/H.03.36.06.18(01); 103 (lower): Grand Pré/PC/Cattroll/H.03.36.03.02(01); 104 (top): Halifax Citadel/PC/L. Cave/H.03.32.09.01(11); 104 (middle): Citadel/PC/H.03.32.09.01(13); 104 (bottom): Learning Resources & Technology, Maritime Museum of the Atlantic; 105 (middle): pilot whale/PC/Cornellier/03.30.10.03(09); 105 (bottom): Citadel/PC/Guindon/H.03.32.06.09(11); 111 (upper): Cape Breton Highlands/PC/St-Jacques/03.30.03.15(22); 111 (middle): Cape Breton Highlands/PC/Cornellier/03.30.03.01(140); Cape Breton Highlands/PC/St-Jacques/03.30.03.25(21); 129 (top, right): Tourism Northwest Territories/M. Milne; 129 (ferry), 132 (quill art): Tourism N. W. T./E. Borke; 129 (bottom, left): Tourism N. W. T./W. Weber; 130 (top/bottom, left), 131 (top): Tourism N. W. T./D. Walker; 130 (middle/bottom, right): Tourism N. W. T./D. Heringa; 132 (bottom, left): Tourism N. W. T./G. Singer; 133 (upper): Tourism N. W. T./A. Kaylo; 133 (lower): caribou/PC/W. Lynch/11.112.10.01(09); 136–137 (inuksuk): Nunavut Tourism/Beedell; 139 (inuksuk): Nunavut Tourism/Heringa; 140 (upper): Nunavut Tourism; 140 (polar bears): Nunavut Tourism/W. Spencer; 144 (top): White Pass & Yukon Route Railroad/C. Racich; 144 (2nd from top): WP&YR/J. Greenberg; 144 (bottom): WP&YR; 145 (upper): *S. S. Klondike*/PC/Cattroll/H.11.37.08.02(53); 145 (lower): *S. S. Klondike*/PC/Cattroll/H.11.37.08.02(103); 146 (upper): Kluane N. P./PC/Beedell/11.110.07.04(30); 146 (lower): Kluane N. P./PC/Lynch/11.110.09.07(27); 147 (left): grizzly bear/PC/Lynch/11.110.10.01(01); 147 (middle): bald eagle/PC/Lynch/07.70.10.02(02); 147 (right): lynx/PC/T. W. Hall/11.110.10.01(14); 148 (top): gold nuggets/PC/H.11.18.05.05(31); 148 (bottom): Dawson City/PC/Butterill/H.11.18.05.05(61); 149 (top, left): Dredge No. 4/PC/Lynch/H.11.22.09.02(30); 149 (middle, left): Palace Grand Theatre/PC/Lynch/H.11.12.01.17(10); 149 (middle, right): Dawson City Post Office/PC/Butterill/H.11.08.06.09(10); 149 (bottom): Dawson City/PC/Butterill/H.11.18.06.09(20); 151 (top): Robert Service Cabin/PC/Butterill/H.11.13.06.11(20); 151 (bottom): polar bear/PC/Lynch/12.123.10.01(16). All maps pieces appearing on pages by MapArt (©MapMedia Corp.). All stamps reproduced courtesy of Canada Post Corporation.
* PC = © Parks Canada

Manufactured by Sheck Wah Tong Printing Press Ltd. Manufactured in Guang Dong, China in October 2009 Job #45646
A   B   C   D   E   F

LETTER FROM THE AUTHOR (4)

INTRODUCING. . .THE TRIP! (5)

BRITISH COLUMBIA (6)

ALBERTA (20)

SASKATCHEWAN (32)

MANITOBA (42)

ONTARIO (52)

QUEBEC (68)

PRINCE EDWARD ISLAND (84)

NEW BRUNSWICK (90)

NOVA SCOTIA (100)

NEWFOUNDLAND & LABRADOR (112)

NORTHWEST TERRITORIES (126)

NUNAVUT (134)

YUKON (142)

WE DID IT! (154)

IT'S THE FACTS! (156)

INDEX (159)

You can grab a map and follow along on our trip.

Bring out the cake and candles!
We're celebrating the 10th anniversary of this award-winning book.

Ten years ago, Guy and Rachel hit the road with their parents for a fictional trip across Canada. From the monster banana slugs of the West Coast to the insect-devouring plants of Newfoundland and north to the shaggy muskoxen of the Arctic—they saw it all. Since then, more than a hundred thousand readers have come along for the ride. The car is getting crowded, but hey—Canada is big enough for everyone!

I've been knocked over by the reaction to this book. Ten years old and still going strong! I once met a boy in Toronto who could recite whole chunks of it from memory. I autographed a copy in Vancouver that was so well-thumbed, loved, and dog-eared it barely held together. Hundreds of copies have crossed the country in kids' backpacks or backseats of cars. Students use it in school classrooms to learn about this country—bad jokes and all. Canadians have sent it all over the world to show other kids what makes this vast country so… wow!

We've made a few updates for this 10th-anniversary edition. Fixed a couple of names that have been changed. Discovered that Brandon, Manitoba, no longer hosts an International Pickle Festival (darn!). But the country hasn't changed much since I dragged my own kids from coast to coast to coast to do the research for this book.

Now it's your turn to pack your bags. Have a grand trip!

Vivien Bowers

(P.S. Send a postcard.)

"Anyone seen my sunglasses?"

Introducing . . . the Trip!

Our whole family is going on a trip across Canada. My parents said we have to do it now because in two years I'll be fourteen and "cool," and I won't want to go anywhere with my family.

"A trip across Canada? Will it be fun? Are you sure it's not going to be educational?" I've learned it pays to ask these things in my family. My mom used to be a teacher, and she can't always turn it off.

"Really fun," my parents answered together. Mom paused a moment. "And nothing educational about it."

"This is a plot so Guy doesn't spend all summer inside playing computer games, isn't it?" said my younger sister, Rachel. She's ten, and she thinks she knows everything.

"We hadn't even considered that," said Dad.

Yeah, right.

Rachel wants to know how far we'll be going. Dad tells her it's about 6,000 km (3,730 miles) across Canada, not including trips to the northern territories on our way back.

"Hey, maybe I'll find some rocks for my rock collection," Rachel announced. She has about a million different collections.

"Very small rocks, I hope," said Dad. "What are you going to collect, Guy?"

"Wildlife. I'm bringing my binoculars. I'd like to see at least one new animal in every province. Preferably charging at the car," I added.

"Then you won't need your binoculars after all," Rachel answered. "I'm bringing Bucko, my stuffed beaver. He's been wanting to see more of Canada, since he is our national animal."

My parents gave us each a journal. Mom said, "You should bring your drawing materials, Guy."

"You could draw a cartoon about Bucko Beaver's trip across Canada," Rachel suggested.

"Dumb idea, Rachel," I said.

On the other hand. . .

Guy

HELP! I'M TRAPPED IN HERE WITH A CRAZY FAMILY.

Warning: Canadian content.

Fluffy. Who is NOT coming with us.

Bucko Beaver is ready for the trip.

Look out, Canada. Here we come.

Are we there yet?

Very funny.

On this great Canadian adventure, we will be crossing the country from west to east. Dad says that because we'll be travelling the same way the Earth is spinning, we'll get some momentum. He also says we need to catch up to the Atlantic Ocean, which got a head start and is 6,000 km (3,730 miles) ahead of us. Very funny. (Some advice: Don't believe everything my dad says!)

Anyway, we are starting our trip in the country's most western province, British Columbia. Warning: British Columbia is quite a long name to write and say, so I, like most Canadians, will be shortening it to B.C.

Welcome to the West!
Welcome to B.C.

Provincial Arms

Provincial Flower
Pacific Dogwood

Provincial Flag

BRITISH

STORMS INCOMING

Queen Charlotte Islands (Haida Gwaii)

Georgia Strait

MAKE WAY! MONSTER LOGGING TRUCKS

Vancouver Island

OUR CAR AT THE STARTING LINE

Nanaimo

Pacific Ocean

RIP

B.C.'S CAPITAL CITY

GRAVEYARD OF THE PACIFIC

Victoria

Juan de Fuca Strait

The Pacific Coast: Good Weather

We are now looking at the Pacific Ocean, on the west side of Vancouver Island, in the province of British Columbia, in the country of Canada, on the continent of. . . You get the picture. This is the official start of our cross-Canada epic journey. I officially dipped my big toe in the Pacific Ocean. It is officially wet.

We're camped on the longest sand beach I've ever seen. This morning Rachel and I raced from our tent way down to the ocean, running through flocks of seagulls that flew up like big white clouds. Then we raced way back in again, chased by huge breakers. Huge, *freezing cold* breakers, I should add. The kind that attack you from behind and bowl you over. Now I've got sand in both ears.

This is Long Beach, where I officially dipped my toe in the water—and became officially excited about our trip.

Stowaway!

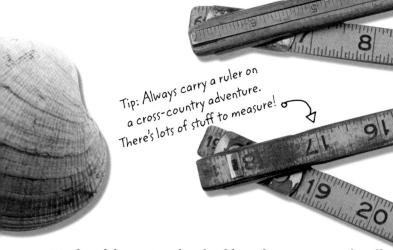

Tip: Always carry a ruler on a cross-country adventure. There's lots of stuff to measure!

Exceedingly Weird

In Nanaimo, on Vancouver Island, there is a bathtub race on the ocean every summer. The racers use souped-up bathtubs with motors on them. The race is 58 km (36 miles) long, and the winners usually do it in about an hour and a half. The losers? They sink.

We found long strands of rubbery brown seaweed, called kelp, washed up on the sand. The longest piece we found was about 8 m (26 ft.). (That's about as long as Rachel and I, toe to toe, three times.) We discovered that if we stomped on the round bulbs, we could make them explode. So we did. Many times.

Rachel found a dead sea star washed up on the beach. Naturally, she wanted to keep it and bring it along with us. Mom said she couldn't because the sea star would stink. (Rachel told me that she might sneak it inside her backpack anyway. She thinks Mom will never find out. Right, Rachel.)

This afternoon we could hear sea lions barking on the rocks offshore. "Oh shut up," we yelled, but they wouldn't. From such a distance, we thought they looked like big, blubbery sausages with flippers. Then we looked at them through our binoculars. They still looked like big, blubbery sausages with flippers. First sighting for my wildlife list!

This is a chiton (pronounced 'kite-on').

Guy's Wildlife List
Sea lion

9

The Pacific Coast: Bad Weather

Exceedingly Weird

Here are a few wacky facts I learned about some of the critters we've seen in and around the water here.

1. Barnacles sit upside down with their heads glued to rocks.

2. Snails, limpets, and chitons all glob onto rocks with a sticky foot. Once they put their foot down, there's no budging them.

3. When a sea otter wants to eat a sea urchin, it floats on its back, uses its tummy as a table, and whacks open the urchin with a rock. (Don't try this at the dinner table.)

4. Seagulls open shells by dropping them from the sky so they smash open on the rocks. Seagulls make big messes.

Goodbye, sunny weather. Today, the wind was really howling. We could lean right against it and not fall over. When it started to rain, the rain blew sideways! Because the weather here comes straight off the Pacific Ocean, it's pretty wild. But at least we're on land. Mom says there's a rocky beach along the coast where many ships have run aground and been wrecked on the rocks during storms. It's called "The Graveyard of the Pacific." Scary.

To escape the rain, we went for a walk in—what else?—a rainforest. All the rain here on the west coast makes terrific rainforests. Everything grows and grows, and when it dies, it rots like crazy. In a rainforest, rotting is good.

"Like walking through a giant compost heap," says Dad. That explains the smell.

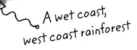

A wet coast, west coast rainforest

The trees are so big! They are hundreds of years old, partly because it's too wet for forest fires here. Lichen hangs like cobwebs from the branches. Huge ferns and new trees sprout from the old rotting dead trees. Soggy moss grows on everything.

Best of all, there are monster banana slugs. I guess they're called banana slugs because they are yellow. They are gigantic! The longest one we could find was 19 cm (7 ½ in.) long—about as long as my whole foot!

"No," said Mom, before Rachel even had a chance to ask. This time I was on Mom's side.

Rainforest

A Canadian rainforest (no monkeys, though).

Food I Was Introduced to for My Own Good

When we visited a small town called Ucluelet (you pronounce that 'you-clue-let'), we bought a salmon from a fish boat at the town dock. Dad wrapped the salmon in aluminum foil and cooked it over our campfire. It was so good, I gave it five stars! Mom cooked oysters. Rachel liked them. My rating . . . well, let's just say I agreed to disagree. We each kept one of the oyster shells.

The ferry (with on-board video arcade!) that took us from Nanaimo to Vancouver.

SALE

BRITISH COLUMBIA FERRY CORP

SPIRIT OF VANCOUVER ISLAND

BC FERRIES

SEE REVERSE SIDE OF TICKET

Here's the sea wall. Watch out for waves at high tide!

Note: The city of Vancouver is not on Vancouver Island. This is very confusing. Someone should fix this.

Vancouver

I now have a scraped elbow and a sore. . . well, let's just say I'm sore all over. Maybe in-line skating isn't my thing. But how could I expect that a huge wave would splash me on the Stanley Park sea wall path just as I got up speed? My whole family was on skates, but next thing I knew I was the only one sprawled in a puddle. Mom says people always get wet in Vancouver because it rains so much, but it takes real talent to get drenched on a sunny day.

The sea wall path goes all around the edge of Stanley Park, right beside the ocean. When I wasn't falling into puddles, I counted seventeen freighters anchored in the bay, alongside sailboats and sailboards. Later, at the port, we watched huge orange cranes unloading containers of stuff from freighters from Japan and Taiwan.

We skated up to some totem poles. Mom said they were built by the Squamish people, Native Canadians who lived here before anyone else.

You can really look up to totem poles.

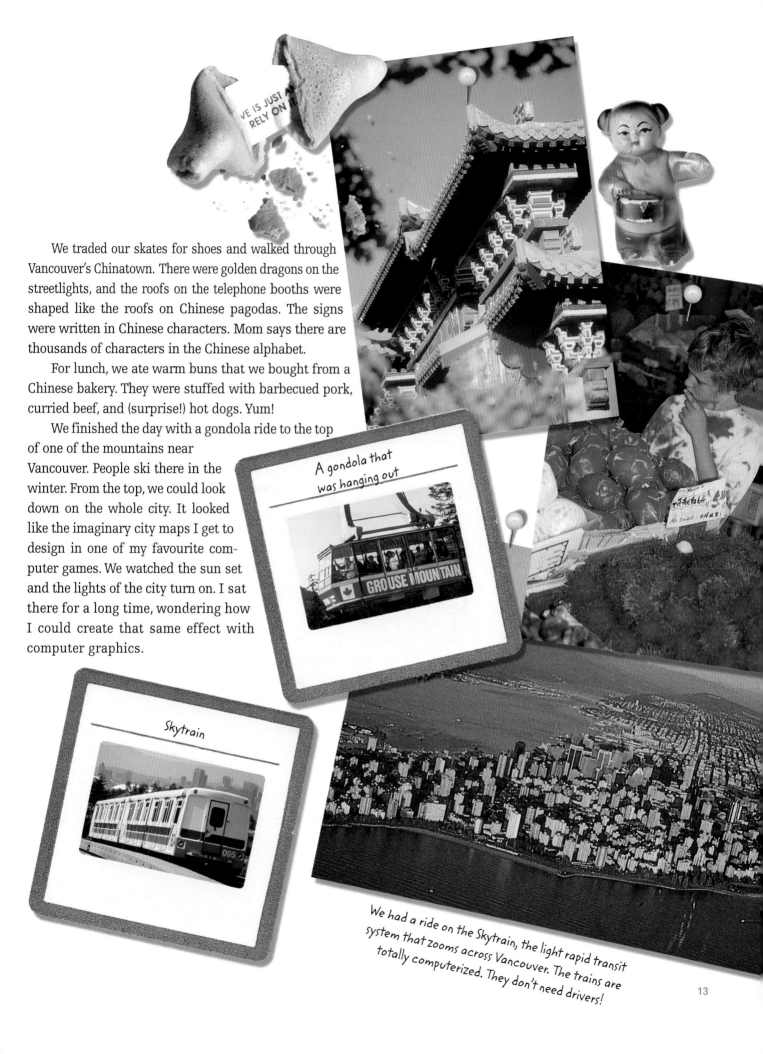

We traded our skates for shoes and walked through Vancouver's Chinatown. There were golden dragons on the streetlights, and the roofs on the telephone booths were shaped like the roofs on Chinese pagodas. The signs were written in Chinese characters. Mom says there are thousands of characters in the Chinese alphabet.

For lunch, we ate warm buns that we bought from a Chinese bakery. They were stuffed with barbecued pork, curried beef, and (surprise!) hot dogs. Yum!

We finished the day with a gondola ride to the top of one of the mountains near Vancouver. People ski there in the winter. From the top, we could look down on the whole city. It looked like the imaginary city maps I get to design in one of my favourite computer games. We watched the sun set and the lights of the city turn on. I sat there for a long time, wondering how I could create that same effect with computer graphics.

A gondola that was hanging out

GROUSE MOUNTAIN

Skytrain

We had a ride on the Skytrain, the light rapid transit system that zooms across Vancouver. The trains are totally computerized. They don't need drivers!

The Mountains

Yesterday Mom and Dad decided we were going to "explore" a mountain. (They're sneaky and never use the word "hike." We always "explore.") We drove high into the mountains on a bouncy gravel road. Then we wrapped a chicken-wire fence around the car. Oh, should I explain? Otherwise porcupines might chew the car's rubber tires and rubber brake hoses (they like the salt).

Then we started along the trail. Dad pointed out places in the meadow where grizzly bears had dug big holes. They use their long, sharp claws to search for yummy roots and small animals to munch. After that, Rachel didn't want to be first on the trail anymore.

We also heard a really high kind of whistle, which Dad said came from a pika, a small animal that looks like a guinea pig. Rachel kept doing pika imitations until it drove me crazy. Mom pointed out that the noise would warn the grizzlies of our approach, so I stopped complaining.

According to Mom

Mom can't help it. She has to tell us things. Here's what she told us about glaciers after we got back to the car.

1. Perfectly preserved bodies of woolly mammoths, extinct for thousands of years, have been found in glacier ice. People have been able to cook up and eat mammoth steaks.

2. Tiny wiggly iceworms actually live in glaciers near the Pacific Coast. They squirm up to the surface to feed on wind-blown pollen or algae.

3. When a glacier flows over a bump, the surface ice can crack open. The crack, or crevasse, can be shallow—or hundreds of metres deep. Mountaineers travelling on glaciers rope themselves together so that if one falls in a crevasse the others can pull him or her out.

There are lots of bears and lots of mountains in this province.

On a glacier.
Watch out for crevasses.

Finally, we scrambled over the last of the rocks and we were on snow—in summer! Mom started explaining how glaciers are formed when snow piles up year after year and never has a chance to melt. But Rachel and I were more interested in sliding down a snow slope.

When we finally settled down to munching peanut-butter-and-jam sandwiches at the edge of the glacier, I complained about the long hike down to the car. Mom said we wouldn't have to hike. A glacier actually flows downhill a little bit each day. We could ride the glacier down to the bottom. All we would have to do is sit here on the snow for a few thousand years. I pointed out that Rachel wouldn't be able to sit still for that long. So we hiked down, and it took almost a thousand years, anyway.

IT'S THE YEAR 11,999. HUGE SHEETS OF ICE, HUNDREDS OF METRES THICK, ADVANCE FROM THE NORTH. CANADA IS HEADED FOR ANOTHER ICE AGE.

IS CANADA DOOMED TO LOOK LIKE ANTARCTICA? PERHAPS NOT! A FAMILIAR FIGURE STREAKS DOWN MOUNT ROBSON, LEAPING OVER THE CREVASSES AND ICE FALLS.

SNOUT TO SNOUT WITH ADVANCING GLACIERS, BUCKO BEAVER REALIZES THERE IS ONLY ONE WAY TO HALT THIS SLOW MOVEMENT OF ICE. THE ULTIMATE WEAPON—THE QUADRUPLE B! (BUCKO BEAVER'S BAD BREATH.)

BUCKO'S AMPLE SUPPLY OF HOT AIR MELTS BACK THE GLACIERS.

THE ICE RETREATS TO THE HIGH MOUNTAIN TOPS, LEAVING BEHIND PUDDLES AND... WHAT'S THIS? A FROZEN PEANUT-BUTTER-AND-JAM SANDWICH! IT HAS APPARENTLY BEEN PERFECTLY PRESERVED IN GLACIAL ICE FOR OVER 10,000 YEARS.

The Hydro Dam— and "Avalanche!"

According to Dad

Dad says that Revelstoke Dam on the Columbia River is big. The W. A. C. Bennett Dam on the Peace River in northern B.C. is bigger. But Canada's biggest hydroelectric-generating dam is the James Bay Project, built on the rivers flowing into James Bay in northern Quebec. The spillway is three times as high as Niagara Falls!

To: kheisler@relay.com
From: gbowers@galaxy.com
Subject: Yo, Kyle!

Hi Kyle,

We are staying with friends in Revelstoke, so I am using their computer to send e-mail. So . . . how's it going?

Believe it or not, Rachel and I are actually still surviving being stuck in the backseat of the car together. Of course, it's much better when she's asleep.

Today we went to a power dam. Now I'm a dam expert. You can ask me any dam questions you want. That's what the guide said today. I'll bet that's his favourite line with tourists.

The dam we visited is on the Columbia River. (Surprise! That's where the "Columbia" part of British Columbia comes from.) We took an elevator all the way up to a lookout at the top of the dam. What a view! On one side of the lookout, we could see the lake, which reached almost to the top of the dam. You would think that the weight of the lake might push over the dam, but that dam is no push-over! It's made of concrete and is really heavy and strong. We looked waaaaay down the concrete slope on the other side of the dam, where the water flows out to the river below. Now that would be some waterslide!

Next we headed down to the powerhouse. That's where the generators are using the energy of the falling water to create electricity. We saw them whirling around, and I couldn't believe how big they were! Each one was about 30 m (almost 100 ft.) across—about the width of five vans parked end to end!

At the visitor's centre we picked up some talking wands. I had a good time walking all around the displays with my friendly wand, listening to the information that was broadcast out of the little speakers on it. Apparently, somebody once dropped a wand off the top of the dam. Amazingly, Rachel didn't.

Catch you later,
Guy

Rogers Pass. Imagine trying to build a road through here.

Our parents have discovered how to keep us quiet in the car—car snacks !

Too Cool to Leave Out

After we left the dam, we drove through steep mountains at a place called Rogers Pass. We passed lots of these gun mounts along the highway. We found out that in the wintertime, the army puts 105 mm (4 inch) howitzer guns on them. The roads are closed, and the guns are fired at the steep slopes high on the mountains. When the gun shells explode, the shock waves shake the snow that has built up on the slopes. Presto! Instant avalanche—and no one is hurt! It's safer to get rid of the snow this way, instead of waiting until a natural avalanche falls on unsuspecting motorists. The railway, however, gave up the snow fight long ago. It goes through a long tunnel under the mountains instead of going along the mountain-sides. The view isn't half as good, though.

Guy's Family Car Trip Survival Tips

I've discovered a foolproof way to pass time and keep my brain active when we have to spend long hours in the car: I write down new and different ways for kids to drive their parents crazy! Here are a few.

1. Sleep your way through Canada's most spectacular scenery.
2. Ask if anyone else can hear that strange thunking noise coming from the engine.
3. Make up another language while in the car. Speak it all day. Answer questions only in this language.
4. Plead with your parents to play mini-golf wherever you go. It will drive them nuts thinking they have brought you to all these wonderful places and all you want to do is play another round of mini-golf.

Goodbye, B.C.

One province down—nine more provinces and three territories left to go! Mom says that once we're through the Rockies, it's all downhill to the Atlantic Ocean. Rachel thinks we're nearly there. She's in for a surprise.

Killer whale

A Steller's Jay feather

ATTENTION

ANIMALS ON ROAD

Things We'll Do and Places We'll Go Next Time

1. Go whale watching off Vancouver Island.

2. See the life-sized mammoth in the Royal British Columbia Museum in Victoria.

3. Sail around the Gulf Islands, between Vancouver Island and the mainland, and maybe see killer whales and porpoises.

4. Go underground at Vancouver's Storyeum for a quick time warp through 400 years of B.C. history.

5. Take a ferry ride up the coast to Bella Coola or Prince Rupert.

6. Go kayaking around the Queen Charlotte Islands.

7. Drive or take the train up the narrow Fraser Canyon.

8. Take the air tram ride over Hell's Gate rapids.

9. Search for the mythical Ogopogo monster in Okanagan Lake.

10. Visit reconstructed longhouses at the 'Ksan Indian Village at Hazelton.

11. Explore 1860s gold-rush towns, like Barkerville.

12. Drive up the Alaska Highway.

13. Come in the winter and go skiing.

14. Play more mini-golf.

Next time, we'll definitely go to Sparwood and see the World's Largest Dump Truck.

I'm being attacked by a wild rose.

How terrifying.

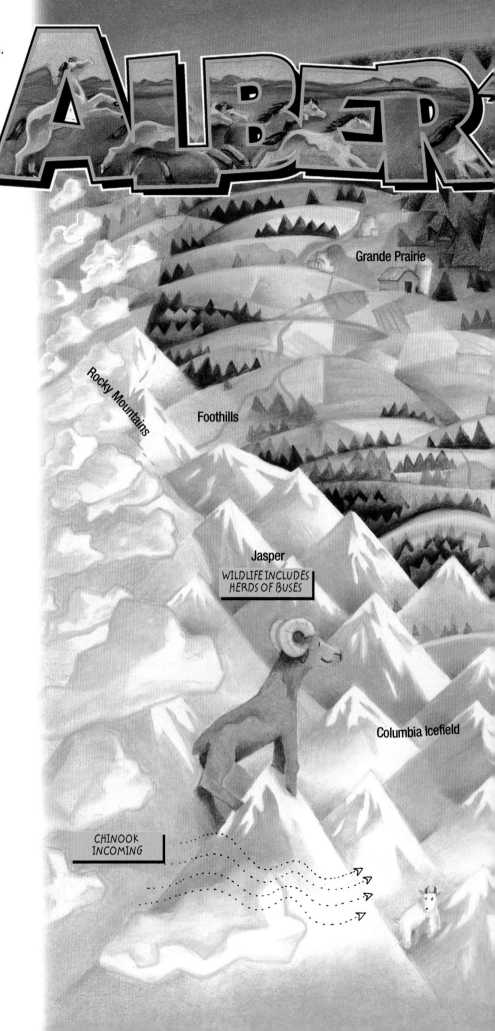

ALBERTA

Grande Prairie

Rocky Mountains

Foothills

Jasper

WILDLIFE INCLUDES
HERDS OF BUSES

Columbia Icefield

CHINOOK
INCOMING

Giddy-up! We've crossed the border into Alberta. Alberta is one of the prairie provinces. That means once we're out of the Rocky Mountains, the land will become flat. Dad says the rich soil is great for growing wheat. There are also lots of cattle ranches here. Mom read that Alberta has more horses than any other province in Canada. So she's singing an old cowboy song while Rachel is bouncing up and down on a pretend horse in the backseat of the car. Dad is adding his pathetic version of a horse whinnying.

Well, if you can't beat 'em, join 'em. "Giddy-up! Giddy-up! Ya-hoo!"

WELCOME TO
ALBERTA
WILD ROSE COUNTRY

INFORMATION CENTRE 4 KM

Provincial Arms

Provincial Flower
Wild Rose

Provincial Flag

TAR SANDS

Edmonton

Red Deer

Drumheller

TYRRELL MUSEUM

BEWARE OF THE
BADLANDS

Dinosaur Provincial Park

Calgary

Banff

ELK HANG OUT ON
STREET CORNERS

OIL WELLS
EVERYWHERE

Head-Smashed-In
Buffalo Jump

WINDMILLS HERE

A real ski jumper (not me!). Okay, let go now. Let go now! Let goooo . . .

Calgary

Giddy-up!

We got the windiest view of Calgary today. The Winter Olympic Games were held here in 1988. A ski jump was built for the event, which is now the highest spot in the city. This morning, we stood at the top of it —and almost got blown off! We pretended we were ski jumpers and looked way, way down to the landing slope below. I made a big decision: Ski jumping is not my thing.

Then we rode the C-Train into downtown Calgary. We took the elevator to the top of the Suncor Energy Centre. It's 52 floors high! (And you wonder why we took the elevator?)

Back at street level, we headed to the Glenbow Museum. What a dynamite exhibit! I'm serious—in the section about oil and gas I got to set off a dynamite charge. I also turned a drill bit, the

The C-Train
Now you "C" it, now you don't.

For ten days each summer, downtown Calgary turns into the Wild West. The Calgary Stampede is a big, wild rodeo with bucking broncos and lots of people wearing cowboy hats.

A pumpjack!
(See? Doesn't that look
like a horse's head?)

thing that drills underground to where the oil hides. Rock is hard to drill through, but it's worth the effort—there's lots of oil under Alberta. Some early Albertans made the first lucky strike just south of Edmonton. Then oil wells started appearing everywhere. My dad said that Alberta went from being a sleepy prairie province with farms and dirt roads to a giant oil patch with 52-storey skyscrapers.

Now we're leaving Calgary, driving on dead-straight roads beside prairie fields. We're watching pump-jacks, machines that help pump oil out of the ground. They look like horses' heads nodding slowly up and down. We also saw a derrick set up to drill into rock in search of oil. During drilling, a kind of chemical mud is pumped down the pipe. It makes things cool (so the drill doesn't overheat) and slippery (so the drill keeps moving smoothly). This is about the muckiest, guckiest job there is. No wonder the workers are called "rig pigs."

According to Dad

How to find oil and get rich quick

1. Figure out where the oil is. Oil is made from very dead, very squished plants and animals that have been buried for 250 million years or so. To find it, you need to look far underground.

2. Drill a test hole into the oil zone.

3. Get a lucky strike. When oil gushes, set up a derrick and drill a well. Get very gucky.

4. When the oil stops gushing, pump the rest of it out.

5. Send your oil through the nearest pipeline to the refinery. Collect wads of money.

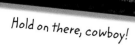

Hold on there, cowboy!

In Calgary, you're never too young to wear a cowboy hat.

23

Head-Smashed-In Buffalo Jump and Writing-on-Stone Provincial Park

Buffalo alert!

Cool name, huh? Head-Smashed-In Buffalo Jump. It's a real place we visited today. Although, actually, the name Buffalo Jump isn't accurate. The buffalo didn't jump; they fell. Back when there were lots of buffalo, and before you could buy your meat shrink-wrapped in cellophane at the supermarket, the Blackfoot people used to stampede buffalo over the cliff so they would fall to their deaths. It provided food for the Blackfoot —and a new winter wardrobe too!

The museum here is built into the cliff. There are some big stuffed buffalo on top of the cliff that look like they're about to leap off. It's so realistic, Rachel refused to stand underneath, just in case. Outside, we walked along trails through the tall grass above and below the cliffs. The guide explained how this place got its name. As the buffalo were driven over the cliff above, a young Blackfoot man was standing underneath, sheltered by a ledge. He became trapped between the pile of buffalo bodies and the cliff. Then the huge pile began to squash him. Later, his people found him with his skull crushed by the buffalo bodies. I guess the moral is: Don't mess with plummeting buffalo.

Tonight we are camped at Writing-on-Stone Provincial Park. Yup, you guessed it. There's lots of writing and carving on the stone around here—in fact, there's more in this park than anywhere else in North America. The pictographs, which are painted on the rock, and petroglyphs, which are carved into the rock, were created by Native people who lived or travelled through this area 3,000 years ago.

Our tent is right beside the Milk River. Tonight Rachel and I had a huge water fight. We used squirters, water bottles, and eventually big buckets! We all got soaked and covered with mud. Now that's fun!

Ever heard of a chinook?
It's a Native word meaning "snow eater."
Chinook winds are strong, warm winds that
can blow through Alberta in the middle of
winter and make temperatures soar!

This sign isn't kidding!
Our car almost got blown off the road!

We saw a rattlesnake near our campsite.

Food I Was Introduced to
for My Own Good

Alberta is beef-ranching
country, so we ate BIG beef
steaks for supper. They were
good, although I actually
prefer my beef in a tube shape
with ketchup and mustard.

Birds of Prey and Dinosaurs

According to Mom

Mom wanted to rap about raptors even after we left the Birds of Prey Centre. She says:

1. An eagle can see a mouse 3 km (2 miles) away. An owl can hear a mouse step on a twig up to 23 m (75 ft.) away. (I'm glad I'm not a mouse.)

2. Falcons are the experts at fast-food take-out. In a dive, they can reach 180 km (112 miles) an hour. They surprise their dinner by approaching low, then sweeping up and over. The falcon usually hits its prey with its feet to stun it. Then it sweeps back to pick it up.

3. According to Native tradition, the eagle has special powers. Because it can fly so high, it is thought that it is a special messenger of the Great Spirit.

Yesterday, we met Mr. Bogle. He's very big, very grouchy—and can turn his head right around backwards! He's at the Alberta Birds of Prey Centre, and he's a great horned owl (Alberta's provincial bird). When he was just a few days old, his tree and nest were cut down. At the centre, they look after injured and orphaned owls, hawks, falcons, and eagles. A lot of birds nest in farmers' fields and often their nests are destroyed by farm machinery at seeding time. I liked the owls best. They kept looking at us, tilting their heads first to one side, then the other.

Rachel's favourite bird was the little American kestrel, or sparrow hawk. We also saw red-tailed hawks and prairie falcons.

Birds of prey are also called raptors. Dad explained that there are lots of raptors on the prairies because there are no trees. That means birds of prey can more easily prey on their prey. Sounds like a raw deal for the prey.

Say "cheese," Alex. At least look at the camera, Alex!

Me holding Alex, a tiny burrowing owl. Burrowing owls nest underground in abandoned badger holes. Dad says that there are hardly any burrowing owls left in Canada. Their habitat is disappearing as the wild prairie is turned into farms and cities.

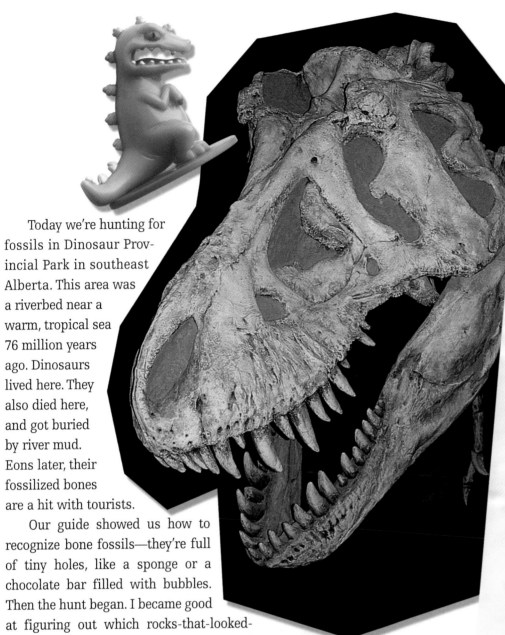

Today we're hunting for fossils in Dinosaur Provincial Park in southeast Alberta. This area was a riverbed near a warm, tropical sea 76 million years ago. Dinosaurs lived here. They also died here, and got buried by river mud. Eons later, their fossilized bones are a hit with tourists.

Our guide showed us how to recognize bone fossils—they're full of tiny holes, like a sponge or a chocolate bar filled with bubbles. Then the hunt began. I became good at figuring out which rocks-that-looked-like-fossils were actually fossils and which ones were simply fossil-like rocks. Rachel found teeth and the fossilized scales of a soft-shelled turtle. I found bones and . . . something else.

"That might be a coprolite, fossilized dinosaur dung," the guide said. "Bite it to see if it's fossilized." No thanks! It may be 76 million years old, but it's still dung!

According to Dad

Paleontologists in Alberta used to think there was a dinosaur called an Albertosaurus. But now that they've found more of them, they've decided that an Albertosaurus is probably just another, slightly different, Gorgosaurus. It's like if aliens came to our planet and met you first. They might think all humans look exactly like you. Then if they met your sister, they might think she was a different species. (You might sometimes think that yourself.) But after seeing lots of humans, all different sizes and shapes, the aliens would probably realize that we are all just slightly different versions of the same thing.

The Great Fossil Seeker at work.

Seen here with our discovery.

BUCKO BEAVER GRABS A CHOCOLATE BAR SNACK. TIME FOR A TRIP BACK IN TIME—75 MILLION YEARS BACK.

AH, THE PERFECT TROPICAL HOLIDAY DESTINATION! LUSH GREENERY, WARM SEAS, EXOTIC BIRDS—A LOVELY SPOT FOR WARP-WEARY TRAVELLERS.

YIKES! HERE COMES A VERY NASTY GORGOSAURUS, LOOKING FOR PLUMP, JUICY MORSELS ON WHICH TO GORGE. BUCKO DECIDES HE'S AT THE WRONG END OF THE FOOD CHAIN AND LEAPS BACK INTO HIS TIME-TRAVEL MACHINE.

75 MILLION YEARS LATER, PALEONTOLOGISTS PUZZLE OVER SOME EXTRAORDINARY CRETACEOUS FOSSILS FOUND IN DINOSAUR PROVINCIAL PARK. COULD IT REALLY BE…A CHOCOLATE BAR?

So Long, Alberta

Things We'll Do and Places We'll Go Next Time

1. Go mountain biking in Kananaskis Country.

2. No hiking required to get to the snow at the Athabasca Glacier! You can ride around on the Columbia Icefield in a special snow-coach with big huge tires.

3. Ride up to 2,200 m (7,220 ft.) on the Jasper Tramway for a great view of the Rocky Mountains. Maybe see a moose, mountain sheep, or elk in Jasper National Park.

4. Mom says that next time, for sure, we'll get to the Royal Alberta Museum in Edmonton.

I want to come back and find more hoodoos. They're like giant mushroom rocks. They have hard rock on top, which hasn't been eroded by water or wind, and soft sandstone underneath, which has been eroded. I had fun going up to them and saying, "How do, Hoodoo?"

Dinosaur skeleton in the Tyrrell Museum, Drumheller, Alberta

CANADA

Dear Brittany:
This is the coolest place!
Humongous dinosaur skeletons and other prehistoric stuff. We watched a paleontologist uncovering a bone fossil from sandstone using a tiny paintbrush and dentist tools. Slow going. He'll probably still be at it if you visit next summer.
Your friend,
Rachel
P.S. Ask Fluffy if she still remembers that she's my cat.

CANADA

Tyrrell Museum

5. Visit Banff National Park, the oldest national park in Canada.

6. Visit Vegreville and see the giant Ukrainian Easter egg. Also visit the Ukrainian Cultural Heritage Village.

7. Visit Edmonton, the capital of Alberta. We'll try to be there to celebrate the Lunar New Year Festival in Chinatown. I'd love to see the firecracker parade and the dragon dance.

"West Edmonton Mall is the largest entertainment and shopping centre in the world!" Rachel read from the brochure. "An important part of Canadian culture!" I agreed when I saw the picture of the gigantic indoor wave pool. We won't miss it next time!

Where Does Popcorn Come From?

"Keep shaking it or it'll burn like last time!" I warned Rachel. We were making popcorn on the campfire. Somehow, it always burns on the bottom.

"I'm sure Aboriginal people burned their campfire popcorn, too," said Dad.

"Who?" asked Rachel.

"Aboriginal people," said Dad. "Native people. The original inhabitants of Canada. Like the Iroquois, the Cree, the Mohawk. . ."

"Where did they get popcorn?" I wondered out loud.

"They grew their own corn and then popped the kernels. Sometimes they dipped it in maple syrup. Later, they introduced popcorn to Europeans who came to Canada," said Mom.

"Keep shaking, Rachel!" I reminded her.

"Europeans learned about growing and eating potatoes and onions from Native people, too," said Dad.

"Not to mention using kayaks and toboggans to get around," Mom said.

"And lots of medicines," Dad added.

"Also place names, such as Canada, Saskatchewan, Ontario, and Moose Jaw," Mom continued.

"I thought a moose had something to do with Moose Jaw," I said.

"Actually, the name comes from the Cree word *moosegaw*, meaning warm breezes," said Mom.

"I smell burning!" Rachel cried.

Later, as we munched handfuls of popcorn, avoiding the burned bits, Rachel said, "I'm confused."

"You usually are," I said.

"I get mixed up with all these different names," she continued. "Blackfoot, Nisga'a, Mi'kmaq, Métis, Inuit. . . It's hard to keep track."

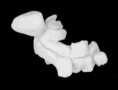

"Well, don't lump them all together. Different Native groups speak different languages and have quite different traditions," explained Mom. "For example, just think about the Blackfoot, who originally lived on the plains, and the Inuit, who live above the treeline in the North. Their lives and cultures must have been very different from each other's."

"Right," Rachel agreed. "Like the Blackfoot probably didn't go whale hunting on the prairies."

"How come we always hear about how Native people lived long ago?" I asked. "If I were a Native person, I think I would find that weird—like I was still supposed to wear moccasins and paddle a canoe."

"Instead of wearing running shoes and driving a pick-up truck," said Dad. "And registering campers in the campground."

"This campground, for example," I said. "James, the guy at the park entrance, told me he's Cree. This is his summer job. In the winter, he's taking university courses to become a teacher."

"Native people drive snowmobiles, send e-mails, act in feature films, design skyscrapers, record hit songs. But that doesn't mean they can't still preserve their heritage also, so they don't lose their traditions, languages, stories, and knowledge about living on the land," said Mom.

"That reminds me. James told me an ancient Cree tradition," said Dad.

"Tell us!" said Rachel.

"He said that long ago, after Cree children would make popcorn over the campfire, they would scour out the bottom of the pan with sand to scrape all the burnt bits off. They would volunteer to wash all the supper dishes. Then they would cheerfully sweep out the tent and. . ."

"Oh, give me a break!" I said.

"How about I give you a scouring pad, instead," suggested Mom, handing it to me.

"It's a flat land after all
It's a flat land after all . . ."

Rachel and I have been singing our Saskatchewan version of the song "It's a Small World After All." The woman at the gas station laughed when Rachel told her Saskatchewan needed a few mountains.

"Oh, you've arrived from out west, eh?" she said. "Those Rocky Mountains are nice, but they sure do get in the way of the view!"

I think I'm going to like Saskatchewan. For one thing, it has nice, straight, tidy boundaries. Also, as the woman joked to Rachel, it's a place where people are outstanding in their field. (Get it?)

Provincial Arms

Provincial Flower
Western Red Lily

Provincial Flag

TCHEWAN
Prince Albert National Park
Batoche National Historic Site
LOUIS RIEL HANGED HERE IN 1885
WHO CALLS?
WHO CALLS?
WHO CALLS?
Regina
POTASH HERE
Qu'Appelle River Valley
Moose Jaw
REALLY BIG JAW-BREAKERS HERE
PRAIRIE DOGS HERE
Grasslands National Park
GOPHERS
Big Muddy Badlands

Cypress Hills

Southern Saskatchewan is amazingly flat. But when people get desperate for trees and hills, they can come here to Cypress Hills. No kidding—real hills. They pop up out of the prairies—sproing! This is the highest point in Canada between Labrador and the Rocky Mountains.

There are also forests of lodgepole pine here (although to me the pine trees look exactly like telephone poles). Actually, the French voyageurs, who travelled here from eastern Canada about 200 years ago, thought the lodgepole pines looked like the jack pines that grow in eastern Canada. *Cypres* is French for jack pine and *montagnes* is French for mountains. So they named this place Montagnes de Cypres. Anyway, now the park is named for a jack pine tree that's not even in the park, and it's too late to change it.

Guy's Wildlife List
Pronghorn antelope

The Great Frog Hunt

Mom says there's a major bird flyway over Saskatchewan. Two million ducks and geese travel between the Arctic and Texas every spring and fall using Saskatchewan's lakes and marshes as stop-over points.

The traffic on this route is awful!

View from the butte.

We walked to the top of Bald Butte for a windy view out onto the prairie. "If you'd stood here 20,000 years ago, you would have been surrounded by ice," said Dad. I'm glad we came today instead.

It turns out that Cypress Hills was one of the only places around that was not totally covered by ice during the last Ice Age, so it has some plants and animals that didn't survive anywhere else.

This afternoon, we looked for leopard frogs in the cattails around the lake. We also saw some pronghorn antelope, which Dad says are the fastest land mammals in North America. They can run up to 100 km (62 miles) an hour. But, hey, never when I'm watching.

After we left Cypress Hills, we drove up to the Great Sand Hills. (No, it just seems that Saskatchewan is all hills!) Rachel and I climbed to the top of the dunes and then leaped down. Fun! That evening, we spent a lot of time trying to get sand out of our hair, our ears, and our noses.

Do you want to pull over and grab a bite to eat in Saskatchewan?

According to Dad

There aren't a lot of trees in southern Saskatchewan. Dad says British Columbia's high mountains block the wet winds coming from the Pacific. To get up and over the mountains, the winds have to dump their water on the west side. By the time the winds reach the prairies, they are dry as a bone.

Grasses can survive such dry conditions because they have lots of roots below and not much plant above. But trees can't survive very well.

Food I Was Introduced to for My Own Good

People in Saskatchewan come from many different ethnic backgrounds. We couldn't decide whether to try traditional Ukrainian breads like paska or babka, German bratwurst, or Russian, Scandinavian, or French food. I figured I could just eat pasta. It's made from durum wheat, and Saskatchewan grows tonnes of it. But Mom said it wasn't very adventurous. In the end, we decided on Saskatoon berries. For hundreds of years, Native people mixed them with dried buffalo meat and melted fat to make a food called pemmican, which would keep a long time. Not us. We gobbled them up in Saskatoon berry pie.

The Prairies

According to Mom

1. Prairie dogs are not man's best friend. They have a nasty habit of destroying his crops. Prairie dogs used to be all over the Saskatchewan prairies—until homesteaders arrived and decimated them to keep their crops safe. Today, they are found only in Saskatchewan's Grasslands National Park.

2. Prairie dogs live in towns of interconnected tunnels and underground chambers, sometimes covering several square kilometres/miles. The towns are divided into "wards" and each ward is divided into "coteries," or small family groups.

3. At the entrance to each burrow is a big mound of dirt. It keeps water from running into the burrow, and it's also where the prairie dog lookout stands. He throws back his head and barks to warn of danger approaching.

4. Prairie dogs nuzzle noses and "kiss" to see if they recognize each other. If they don't, they quit kissing and start fighting instead.

Our car is like some tiny insect beetling across a wide, flat ocean of golden wheat. The farms stretch on and on to the horizon under an enormous blue sky. The grain fields ripple with waves in the wind. When we spot a grain elevator on the skyline, we know there's another tiny settlement up ahead along the railroad tracks.

I like the neat lines made by farm machinery on the fields. It looks like a patchwork quilt. The prairie is very orderly except where a coulee (a dried-up stream bed) makes an unauthorized squiggle through the otherwise perfectly arranged landscape.

As we drive, we're playing the alphabet game—again.

Rachel: "'A' is for . . . air. Now 'B.'"

Guy: "Bison."

Rachel: "What bison? There aren't any. I read that all the bison that used to roam the prairies were shot a long time ago."

Guy: "Okay, we'll use that red barn coming up instead. 'C'?"

Mom: "I can't see a coulee, but there's a field of canola. See that bright yellow field over there?"

A prairie dog

PIONEER

Rachel: "Is canola like granola?"

Mom: "No, it's used to make canola oil. Then we cook with it. What about 'D'?"

Rachel: "How about dirt? Black dirt."

Dad: "Good one. You know, the prairies used to be a lake. Rivers washed a lot of soil into the lake, and when it dried up, it left good clay-like soil for planting."

Mom : "Now 'E.' We can always look for an 'E' on a sign."

Guy: "Okay, are we anywhere near the towns of Elbow, Eyebrow, or Earache?"

Mom: "Earache? Is there an Earache in Saskatchewan?"

Guy: "No, but there should be. There is an Eyebrow and an Elbow."

Rachel: "There's our 'E'! Here comes a grain elevator! Yippee!" And so it goes.

Mom and Rachel checking out the wheat crop.

Sometimes, for a joke, a farmer sticks a pair of pants and boots out the end of a hay bale so it looks like someone's trapped inside!

Lightning storm.
They do them well in Saskatchewan.

A: Where do you live?
 B: Forget.
A: You forget where you live?
 B: No, I live in Forget, Saskatchewan. What about you?
A: Biggar.
 B: Biggar than what?
A: Forget.
 B: You can't remember?
A: No, I live in Biggar, and it's bigger than Forget.

A   B

Oops, Mom says Forget is a French name, pronounced "for-jay."

37

Moose Jaw and Regina

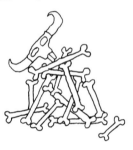

Yesterday we were in Moose Jaw—home to Canada's largest military jet-training base and the Canadian Snowbirds, the aerial acrobatic squadron that performs at air shows. Unfortunately, the Snowbirds were doing somersaults out of town yesterday. Instead, we went to the Western Development Museum and watched them on video in the Snowbirds Gallery. It was awesome, but Rachel's eyes were closed through most of it. She doesn't like flying upside down.

This morning, we reached Regina. We ate a picnic lunch on Willow Island, in Wascana Centre. It's a park that was made out of dry prairie by damming Wascana Creek. Now there's an artificial lake, islands, trees, and ducks that hit up the visitors for snacks. Then we headed to the Royal Saskatchewan Museum. We saw lots of stuffed Saskatchewan wildlife, including prairie dogs. They are cute—a lot cuter than the big, ugly T-rex dinosaur that lunged at me with a horrible roar when I pressed a button!

The RCMP Sunset Retreat Ceremony in Regina

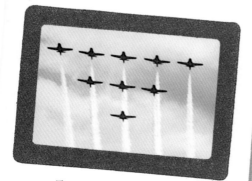

The Snowbirds' Air Show

All day I've been warning Rachel: "Behave yourself. We're in Mountie territory!" The Mounties are the Royal Canadian Mounted Police, or RCMP, Canada's national police force. They were first established in 1873 as the North-West Mounted Police, and their first headquarters were set up in Saskatchewan in 1882. The Mounties' training school is here in Regina. Tonight we're going to watch their Sunset Retreat Ceremony. Mom says to expect a lot of marching, drumming, and shouting of orders before the Mounties lower the flag and go to bed.

To: kheisler@relay.com
From: gbowers@galaxy.com
Subject: Hello from Saskatchewan!

Hey Kyle,
We're staying overnight with relatives in Saskatoon, which means I have access to a computer again. So . . . it looks like you get mail!

Today, the people we're staying with took us to the Wanuskewin (pronounced Wah-nus-KAY-win) Heritage Park, near Saskatoon. Wanuskewin is Cree for "seeking peace of mind." After all the "quality" time I'm spending with my family, peace of mind sounded like a great idea. Rachel had to come too, though, so peace and quiet was hard to find.

We did see how the Cree and other Native people lived here in the days of the buffalo, and ever since. We walked on the trails around the park and saw a tipi ring from a long-ago Native camp and a medicine wheel, which had a cairn in the middle and long strings of rock leading out from there. No one knows if these mysterious medicine wheels were used for ceremonies, or had something to do with astronomy, or were like giant direction signs.

Also, I learned lots of ways to hunt bison—sneaking up on them wearing a wolf skin, herding them over cliffs, or driving them into buffalo pounds. You never know when this knowledge will come in handy! The wild bison are all gone now, but sometimes you can see the old buffalo trails that cross the prairie.

Canada is B-I-G, but I haven't given up hope that I'll be coming home sometime. In the meantime, watch out for stampeding herds of bison!
Catch you later,
Guy

"Is it time to go to Manitoba now?"

Qu'Appelle Valley

Dear Brittany:
We're in the Qu'Appelle Valley. Here the story behind how it got its name: A young Native man was canoeing down the lake to see his bride late one night. He heard some-one call his name. "Qu'appelle?" he called back, which means "Who called?" in French. The only answer was the echo of his words. He finally reached his bride, but she had died earlier that night. Just before she died, she had called his name.

Sad, huh?
Bye, Rachel

Things We'll Do and Places We'll Go Next Time

1. We'll visit places in northern Saskatchewan. Maybe we'll canoe in Prince Albert National Park, raft the Churchill or Clearwater rivers, or visit Athabasca Sand Dunes Provincial Park.

2. We'll stay at a bed-and-breakfast on a grain farm.

3. Mom wants to see a performance of "The Trial of Louis Riel" in Regina.

4. I want to see the prairie dogs along the Frenchman River in Grasslands National Park, as well as the herds of bison.

5. We'll go to a powwow (maybe the Standing Buffalo Indian Powwow at Fort Qu'Appelle in early August or the Chief Poundmaker Memorial Powwow in Cut Knife in July).

6. Dad wants to visit the other Western Development Museums — in Yorkton, Saskatoon, and Battleford.

Qu'Appelle Valley

Wanuskewin Heritage Park

Fort Walsh

"You bet!
Step on the gas
and go-pher it!"

Here's a good car game to play in Saskatchewan. Grab a map of the province and play my latest invention: the Alphabetical Towns Game! There are strings of towns in alphabetical order here. Mom says they are from the days when towns were created and named along the railway line. For instance, in southeast Saskatchewan near Melville, I found Fenwood, Goodeve, Hubbard, Ituna, Jasmine, Kelliher, and LeRoss, all in a row. Looks like they gave up before they reached Q or X, though.

7. I'd like to come to the Saskatchewan Air Show in July that features the Snowbirds. (Mom says that sounds noisy.)

8. Swim at Little Manitou Lake, near Watrous. There's lots of salt and other minerals in the water there. You can float like a cork!

9. Visit the Batoche National Historic Site. There was a major battle here between the Métis (who are people of both Native and European descent) and the government forces during the Northwest Rebellion of 1885.

BUCKO BEAVER RAMS HIS TIME-TRAVELLING GIZMO INTO REVERSE. AVOIDING A NEAR COLLISION WITH THE SNOWBIRDS, HE ZOOMS PAST THE DROUGHT AND DUST STORMS OF THE 1930S—AND BACK INTO PRAIRIE HISTORY.

BB STARES THROUGH THE WINDOW AT TIME MOVING IN REVERSE. PLOUGHS UN-PLOUGH THE FIELDS. PRAIRIE SETTLERS UN-ARRIVE, TAKING THE TRAIN BACKWARDS. THE TRAIN TRACKS THEMSELVES BECOME UNBUILT. VOYAGEURS REVERSE UP RAPIDS.

BB WALKS OUT ONTO WILD, UNCULTIVATED PRAIRIE. AH—SUCH PEACE OF MIND! SUDDENLY THE SILENCE IS BROKEN. THE EARTH IS SHAKING! TAKE COVER, BUCKO!

Dancers at Wanuskewin

Batoche National Historic Site

Lots of very airy prairie out there!

PRAIRIE / CANADIAN SHIELD

For Pete's sake, all rocks and lake!

MAN

We're entering Manitoba, which, so far, looks a lot like Saskatchewan to me. Come to think of it, Saskatchewan didn't look all that different from Alberta.

Hey, do these prairies go on forever?

Mom says they will end eventually. The prairies will be replaced by rocky Canadian Shield country before we leave Manitoba. Yippee!

Dad says if we think the prairies go on forever, wait till we drive through the Canadian Shield!

Uh-oh.

Friendly Manitoba

ADS 179

SEP 99

30

Provincial Flower
Prairie Crocus

Provincial Arms

Provincial Flag

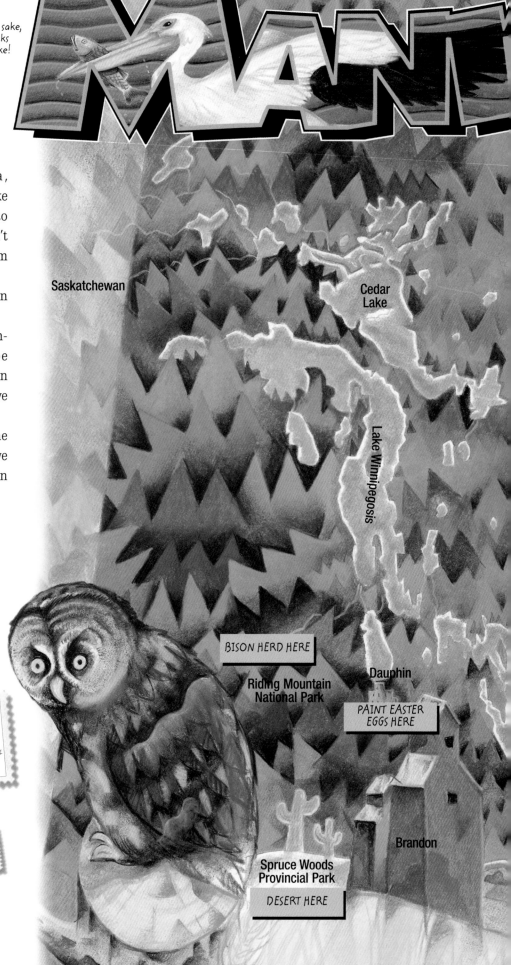

Saskatchewan

Cedar Lake

Lake Winnipegosis

BISON HERD HERE

Riding Mountain National Park

Dauphin

PAINT EASTER EGGS HERE

Brandon

Spruce Woods Provincial Park

DESERT HERE

TOBA
Hudson Bay
Churchill
Nelson River
Thompson
DO YOU MINE?
CANADIAN SHIELD BEGINS
Lake Winnipeg
Grand Beach
Gimli
SNAKES ALIVE!
WELCOME TO NEW ICELAND
Whiteshell Provincial Park
VERY OLD ROCK
Ontario
Oak Hammock Marsh
Winnipeg
Lake Manitoba
Assiniboine River
THE FORKS!
DINOSAURS WERE HERE
Red River

Spruce Woods Provincial Park: Home of the shy skink

Happy Birthday to Me!

What do you know—I'm a teenager today! When I woke up at our campsite at Spruce Woods Provincial Park, the tent was hung with balloons.

"How did I end up with a teenager?" asked Mom. "Has it really been 13 years?"

"Let me count my grey hairs," said Dad.

I made the rule that since it's my birthday today, I get to call the shots. That didn't mean other people set aside their own ideas of what we should do.

"We could walk through the sand dunes and find a skink," said Dad.

"Skink?" I asked. It pays to be suspicious when you're dealing with my dad.

"The northern prairie skink," he said. "It's Manitoba's only lizard, and this park happens to be the only place you can find them in Canada. *If* you can find them. They're shy."

To Guy

Chomp Chomp Chomp Chomp CHOMP! HAPPY BIRTHDAY! (A biting comment from Bucko Beaver.)

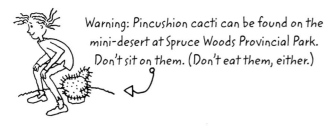

Warning: Pincushion cacti can be found on the mini-desert at Spruce Woods Provincial Park. Don't sit on them. (Don't eat them, either.)

I decided that looking for shy skinks was probably not worth the effort.

"Of course, we might see a hognose snake instead," said Dad.

"A hognose snake?"

"It has a turned-up nose that it uses to dig for toads."

Either the wildlife around here is very weird or my dad is. Possibly both. I decree that this morning we'll ride in the horse-drawn, covered wagon that takes visitors for tours through the sand dunes. (Why walk when there's an alternative?) For the afternoon, we'll check out a waterslide near Brandon that has "137-metre (450 foot) water twisters" (according to the brochure). Then we'll go out to dinner and I'll order anything I want. Then I'll stay up as late as I want.

"That's fine," said Dad. "You can stay up and party with the skinks. I'll be going to bed."

Happy Birthday to my brother
He is stinky like no other
I'm glad I don't have another
Stinky crabby older brother!

From Rachel

P.S. Just kidding!
P.P.S. (No, I'm not. It's true!)

Food I Was Introduced to for My Own Good

Today I had a Manitoban chocolate birthday cake for the first time in my life. It tastes like other birthday cakes I've had—and there's nothing wrong with that!

Exceedingly Weird

Mom and I were looking through the Manitoba Events Guide. Here are some of the wackier summer events Manitoba has hosted.

1. There's an event called the St. Pierre Frog Follies, that features a National Frog Jumping Championship.

2. Islendingadagurinn is an Icelandic festival held in Gimli. I don't know what they do, but they should award prizes for whoever can say "Islendingadagurinn" in one breath.

Islendingadagurinn

3. The Asessippi Model Airplane Show advertised a flying car, a flying lawnmower, and a flying Snoopy doghouse.

Party on, Bucko!

Right you are, hognose snake! Join us, skink?

I'll just sit quietly over here, thank you.

45

Winnipeg

The windiest corner in Canada

The basilica at Saint-Boniface

The Forks

The Royal Canadian Mint

"So where's the wind?" asked Rachel.

We're in downtown Winnipeg—standing at the corner of Portage and Main. Portage Avenue and Main Street is supposed to be the windiest street corner in Canada, but there wasn't even a breeze today. Lots of traffic, but no wind. Maybe if we come back in the middle of winter we'll feel wind. On second thought, cancel that—I've heard about Winnipeg winters! That's why Winnipeg has so many indoor shopping areas. Portage Place, for example, covers about three city blocks.

This morning we toured the Royal Canadian Mint and saw how they make money. They make two billion coins a year, for Canada and for other countries. (No free samples!) We also went to the Manitoba Museum. This is a good museum. It's okay to let your mom drag you there. In the museum we went aboard a full-sized replica of an old ship called the *Nonsuch*. It was the ship that sailed into Hudson Bay in 1668 and loaded up with furs to take back to England. When people there saw those furs, they wanted more! The fur trade started and the Hudson's Bay Company was formed. Which, from the beavers' point of view, was a bad idea.

A: What do you do for a living?
B: I make money.
A: So do most people. But how do you make your money?
B: I make money.
A: You're not making sense.
B: Oh, yes, I make cents. Also nickels, dimes . . .
A: Ah, ha! You work at the mint! You make money!
B: Of course I do. You think I would work for free?

A   B

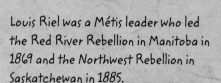

We had lunch in Saint-Boniface, the French part of Winnipeg. Rachel insisted we see the grave of Louis Riel, which is in the graveyard at the big basilica. Riel's the Métis leader who led the Northwest Rebellion. He was born and buried here in Saint-Boniface.

We walked across the bridge over the Red River, which isn't very red, to the Forks. Rachel and I went looking in a restaurant for the forks. Mom interrupted our fork hunt so we could paddle a canoe up the Red River to where the Assiniboine River flows in, creating a "fork" in the river. Aha! The Forks!

Almost every historical thing that's ever happened in Manitoba happened right here at The Forks. If somebody had thought to set up a time-lapse camera starting about 6,000 years ago, they could have recorded a great documentary. Early Native camps, explorers, fur traders, Métis settlements, Scottish homesteaders, the coming of the railway, right up to present-day Winnipeg (the movie could end with the arrival of me—Tourist Extraordinaire!).

According to Mom

Louis Riel was a Métis leader who led the Red River Rebellion in Manitoba in 1869 and the Northwest Rebellion in Saskatchewan in 1885.

Métis means "mixed" in French, and the Métis were called that because they came from a "mixing" of European and Native people (usually French and English traders who married Ojibwa or Cree women). Riel emerged as a leader of his people in their fight with the government of Canada to protect their land, way of life, language, and religion. He was hanged for treason after the Northwest Rebellion.

The rebellions make for interesting history, but if I were Métis, I'd be pretty frustrated by now. According to Mom, the Métis are *still* trying to negotiate land claims with the Canadian government, over a hundred years and two rebellions later. They also want Louis Riel to be officially pardoned.

LOUIS RIEL
1844 ✝ 1885

RIEL

The signs along the Riverwalk explain—in English, French, and Cree—all the things that have happened at The Forks. To pass the time in the car, I could teach myself Cree so I can read the signs.

Home of Louis Riel

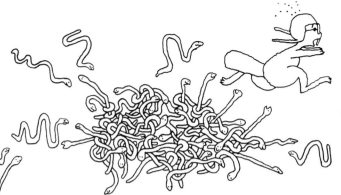

Snakes and Lakes

"That's a red-sided garter snake," said the park interpreter, looking at my snake with its red-and-yellow stripes.

"Totally harmless, right?" said Mom.

"Unless you are a frog or toad."

"Ribbit," said Mom.

The interpreter said we should come back in the spring and visit the snake pits near Narcisse. That's when the snakes do their mating thing.

"You can look down into this huge pit in the ground and see 10,000 wriggling snakes! After a while, your eyes have trouble focusing," he said.

Snakes alive!

It's hot. The temperature was almost 40°C (104°F) yesterday. Luckily, Manitoba has lots of lakes as well as snakes. We're camped at Grand Beach on Lake Winnipeg. The lake is huge, but Dad says it used to be even bigger. It's just part of what used to be the world's largest lake—Lake Agassiz. When the last ice age ended, thousands of years ago, the melting ice filled a lake that covered most of Manitoba. Here at Grand Beach, there's a hill where you can see earth ledges at three different levels. They show the height Lake Agassiz used to be at different times in the past. Once, the hill was actually an island in the middle of the lake.

Spotting birds at Oak Hammock Marsh

Sighting #1
Yellow-headed blackbird

Sighting #2
Red-winged blackbird
in flight

Sighting #3
Red-winged blackbird
sitting still (good)

Sighting #4
Tree swallow

Sighting #5
Pelican on souvenir

Look out—it's the Red River floodway!

Red River Floodway

Don't be fooled by the seagull, or the size of Lake Winnipeg. It is a lake, not the sea!

UNLIKE THE REST OF MANITOBA, BB LIKES IT WHEN THE RED RIVER FLOODS.

Guy's Wildlife List
Richardson's ground squirrel

The park interpreter says Manitoba is lower and flatter than other provinces, so it made a good lake bottom. The water hasn't forgotten that, either. Every spring, rivers rush down into Manitoba on their way to Hudson Bay. Usually the water behaves and stays in the rivers, but sometimes it floods the banks and Manitoba turns into a big puddle again. The Red River floods so often they've built a big canal around Winnipeg so the water will bypass the city and make lakes somewhere else.

Dad's happy because there's a lagoon, plus lots of other good bird-watching places nearby. We went to Oak Hammock Marsh and Netley Marsh on the way here. Rachel and I usually look for white pelicans, but we haven't seen one yet. Instead, at Oak Hammock Marsh, we saw hundreds of Richardson's ground squirrels. They're cute, but they don't fly.

❖CANADA❖

Dear Brittany:

I'm sending this from the Republic of New Iceland. No, we haven't gone off course and ended up in Iceland (yet!). Although nothing would surprise me, with my parents running this show. We're in Gimli, Manitoba. Lots of people here came from Iceland a long time ago, so it's quite Icelandic. There's an Icelandic festival held in Gimli called Islendingadagurinn. The more ice the better, I say. It's so hot!

Your fried friend,
Rachel

Viking Statue, Gimli, Manitoba

Gimli

CANADA

The halfway mark.

Halfway Across!

Things We'll Do and Places We'll Go Next Time

1. We'll go horseback riding in Riding Mountain National Park. It's a good place to howl at the wolves and hear them howl back. There's also a herd of bison there.

2. I want to go to the snake pits in the Narcisse Wildlife Management Area in spring to watch the mating ritual.

3. Rachel wants to go rock-hounding for agate and jasper at the quarry in Souris.

4. We'll go to Churchill in northern Manitoba. It's above the treeline on the coast of Hudson Bay. It's so remote you can't even drive there—you can only get there by train or airplane. It sure sounds like it's worth the 20-hour train ride from Winnipeg, though. I want to go for polar bear season, September or October. The northern lights should be good then, too.

5. Rachel wants to see the Royal Winnipeg Ballet.

6. Dad wants to see the Winnipeg Symphony Orchestra.

7. Mom wants to go to the Winnipeg Folk Festival.

8. I want to see those Frog Jumping Championships!

Believe it or not, we're now half way across Canada. Manitoba is in the middle of the country if you're going from west to east (or east to west). Of course, as Dad reminded me, there's also the north. Canada has lots of north. We *specialize* in north. So, on the other hand, I guess I won't be home playing video games with Kyle anytime soon.

Manitoba has one of the most ethnically diverse populations in Canada, and has lots of festivals to prove it. There's the National Ukrainian Festival in Dauphin, the Icelandic festival in Gimli, and various Native pow-wows. If you want to be efficient, you can celebrate all the different heritages at once at the big Folklorama held in Winnipeg each summer.

From Africa

From Korea

Cool catfish sighted in Selkirk, The Catfish Capital of the World. (Now you know.)

This is a statue of Winnie the Bear in Assiniboine Park in Winnipeg. A soldier from Winnipeg bought him in Ontario and took him to England during the First World War. Winnie ended up in the London Zoo. He was the "bear of little brain" that A. A. Milne wrote about in Winnie the Pooh.

Real prairie is hard to find these days. A real prairie doesn't have wheat fields or 18-hole golf courses. A real prairie is a natural, tall-grass prairie, made up of lots of different native plants. You can walk through some at the Living Prairie Museum in Winnipeg.

Sighting for Mom's "nice old barn" collection.

From Scotland

From Thailand

From Hungary

Ah, this is the life.

ONTARI

THE GROUP OF
SEVEN WAS HERE

Lake of
the Woods

MOSQUITOES
INCOMING!

Thunder Bay

Wawa

BIG GOOSE HERE

Lake Superior

GRAIN
THIS-A-WAY

Sault Ste. Marie

NICKNAMED
"THE SOO"

USA

Lake Michigan

We've entered Ontario! Will we ever get to the other side, though? Ontario is 1,600 km (995 miles) across. I looked at the map, and I think it's also bigger than it's supposed to be from top to bottom. From the west, the border between Canada and the United States follows neatly along the 49th parallel of latitude—but Ontario's border goes berserk! At Point Pelee, in Lake Erie, the border drops *way* down south—so far that cactuses grow there.

"What happened?" asked Rachel. "Did the ruler slip when they were drawing the border?"

Mom says it has nothing to do with slipping rulers. The border was set right through the middle of the Great Lakes in 1783, after the American Revolution.

I guess it's good for tourism. See folks: Canada isn't all just ice and snow!

Provincial Flag

 Provincial Arms

Provincial Flower
White Trillium

North Shore of Lake Superior

Exceedingly Weird

We found this goose in Wawa. Wawa means "wild goose" in the Ojibwa language. Mr. Goose is 9 m (30 ft.) tall and made of steel. The man at the gas station here said that once people in Wawa woke up to find huge goose footprints painted on the Trans Canada Highway. I like a goose with a sense of humour!

According to Mom

Fort William was an important spot in the days of fur trading. Once a year, at a time called the Great Rendezvous, fur trappers working for the North West Company would return to Fort William, their canoes filled with a year's worth of furs to trade with merchants from Montreal. The Great Rendezvous was a huge celebration, which is re-created in Thunder Bay every July. It lasted for weeks, and then the merchants left, bringing the furs out through the Great Lakes to Canada's eastern seaports, where they could be shipped to Europe. Sounds fun . . . unless you were a beaver.

Let's skip the Great Rendezvous this year.

"Rachel, stop! You've been singing the same song all day!" I beg.

"Isn't Lake Superior wild and wonderful?" Mom says. She's trying to distract us so we don't clobber each other in the backseat.

"Big deal," I say.

"Very big," Mom agrees. "In fact, it's the largest freshwater lake in the world."

Hey, how did that become a teachable moment?

We spent the day at Old Fort William, a big North West Company post, in what is now Thunder Bay. We were time-warped back to the year 1815, and helped a voyageur who was building a birchbark canoe. He told us he paddles 16 to 18 hours a day. Rachel thought that was nuts.

"Haven't you heard of speedboats?" she asked. He seemed interested in the idea, but thought they would be really heavy to portage.

We gave a big send-off to a fur brigade that was heading north to take supplies and trade goods to fur-trading posts in the interior. The cannon fired, and everyone waved and cheered as the voyageurs paddled off in the loaded canoe. Then, half an hour later, we saw one of those same voyageurs walking though town in jeans and a T-shirt. (You should have heard Rachel then.)

Tonight we're camping at Lake Superior Provincial Park. Tomorrow, we'll drive and drive to Lake Huron—another Great Lake.

Amethyst

Here's the newest addition to Rachel's rock collection—an amethyst. We went digging for amethysts at an open pit where they gave us buckets and shovels. The more we dug, the hotter we got. Eventually, Mom agreed that the best place to go mining for amethysts was the gift shop.

According to Dad

Since we keep talking about the Great Lakes, we asked Dad exactly what was so great about them. He told us they are five linked lakes, the biggest in a chain of large lakes along the southern border of the Canadian Shield. They are: Lake Superior, Lake Michigan (which is entirely in the United States), Lake Huron, Lake Erie, and Lake Ontario. Since the early days of the fur trade, the Great Lakes have provided an important transportation route into the North American continent. They drop from 183 m (600 ft.) above sea level at Lake Superior to 74 m (242 ft.) at Lake Ontario. The most dramatic drop is at Niagara Falls (stay tuned—we're heading there soon!).

This one is Huron.

Georgian Bay is here.

Georgian Bay

We've been staying for a few days at our friends' cottage on French River, near Georgian Bay, on the north shore of Lake Huron.

On our way here, we went for a (wet) canoe trip in Killarney Provincial Park. We had to do a portage, which means carrying the canoe on our shoulders, which I do not recommend. Not ever, but especially not when the trail is muddy and slippery.

When I complained, Mom asked, "Didn't that voyageur you met in Fort William say he sometimes carried 80 kg (175 lb.) loads over the portages?"

"Well, kilograms weren't as heavy back then," I said.

"Inflation, right?" said Dad. "Kilograms are bigger these days." That sounds logical to me.

On our canoe ride, I collected a moose and some monarch butterflies for my wildlife list. Rachel collected a poison ivy rash, which she has to put cream on three times a day.

According to Dad

We saw monarch butterflies on our canoe trip, and Dad said that must mean there were milkweed plants where we were. That's what they eat. When they are caterpillars, monarchs munch on certain kinds of milkweed leaves that are actually toxic. The poison doesn't bother the monarch caterpillars at all, but it does make them taste bad to predators. That's a good trick!

Monarch butterflies sometimes roost together in large clusters of hundreds or even thousands at the edge of the Great Lakes. They avoid Ontario winters by migrating to Mexico—another good trick.

Guy's Wildlife List
Monarch
butterfly

We were happy to get to our friends' cottage. We spend all day swimming and jumping off rocks. When my friend Dustin and I were snorkelling this afternoon, we found some fish, a snapping turtle (I still have all my toes), and two full cans of pop! In the hottest part of the day we take cover from the sun and play lots of cards and board games. (I am a ruthless game player, so I usually win.)

Mom took the car to the garage today because it's been acting a little tired and cranky. Turns out it needs an oil change and a clutch adjustment. That's ok, I'm not in any big rush to leave here.

The weather has been perfect, but if it turns bad we have a rainy day plan. We'll go to Sudbury for a day. We can visit Science North, which is supposed to be a cool science museum, and the nickel mine. There's an enormous "Big Nickel" that's outside the mine (which Dustin says is actually made of stainless steel). So far, though, it's been too nice to go anywhere.

Now I'm off to hit the sack. From my bed at night, I can hear the loons calling.

According to Mom

Mom asked us if any of the scenery we've been seeing looks familiar to us. Rachel said it reminded her of paintings she saw on a class trip to an art gallery. Mom was thrilled. I guess that was the answer.

Mom told us there's a group of famous early 20th-century Canadian painters called the Group of Seven. (There were seven of them, all living in Toronto, when they started out.) They are known mostly for their paintings of the rugged northern Ontario landscape—the rocks, trees, sky, and water around us right now.

The group showed the Canadian wilderness in a new way. Their paintings had a freer style and the colours they used expressed a lot of feeling for what they painted, which was different from the European style of art that was popular at the time. They are all dead now, but their paintings are still known all over the world.

Toronto is on Lake Ontario.

Toronto

CN Tower

We're in Toronto now, the biggest city in Canada. After our first day here, Dad, Rachel, and I have figured out how to find our way on the subway. We'd make good moles. Not Mom. Every time we climb up to street level from an underground subway station, she's completely confused and heads off in the wrong direction.

We found our way to the best view of Toronto— the top of the CN Tower. We went up there yesterday. The tower is taller than both New York's Empire State Building and the Eiffel Tower in Paris. You go up 342 m (1,122 ft.) in a glass elevator in 58 seconds, and your stomach gets there a few seconds later. Mom told us the speed of the elevators is the same as the rate of ascent of a jet at take-off!

From the top, we looked down on the skyscrapers, the Ontario Parliament Buildings at Queen's Park, and the Rogers Centre, where the Toronto Blue Jays play.

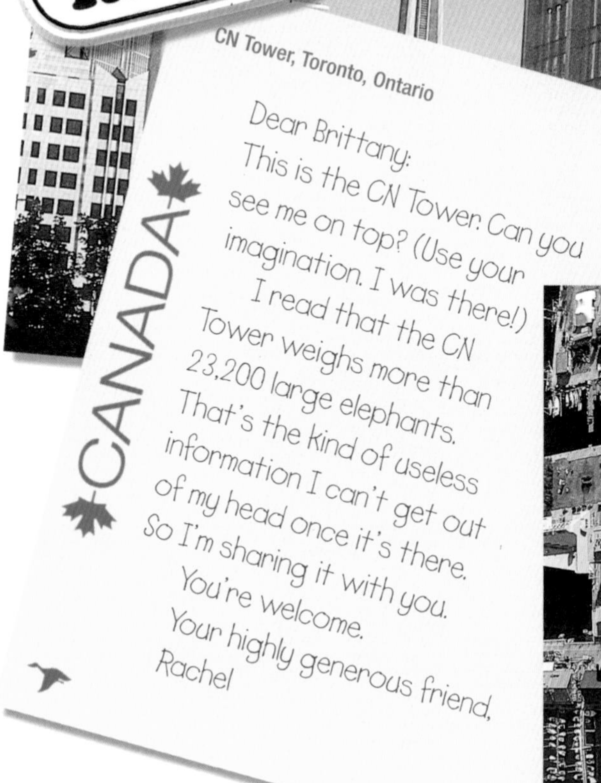

TORONTO

Rachel

CN Tower, Toronto, Ontario

CANADA

Dear Brittany:
This is the CN Tower. Can you see me on top? (Use your imagination. I was there!)
I read that the CN Tower weighs more than 23,200 large elephants. That's the kind of useless information I can't get out of my head once it's there. So I'm sharing it with you. You're welcome.
Your highly generous friend,
Rachel

Three views from the CN Tower, including one past Mom's feet through the glass floor.

Toronto Islands

When we looked south, we saw the harbour and the Toronto Islands in Lake Ontario. The lake seemed to go on forever. While Mom and Dad tried to recognize more landmarks, Rachel and I looked for squirrels. (We've heard there are lots of black squirrels living in Toronto.) They are hard to spot from that far up.

Then the three brave members of our family walked on the tower's glass floor. It's at the top, and you look down to the ground beneath your feet, 113 storeys below. Dad refused to step out onto it, which we thought was hilarious. We eventually shamed him into it, but he didn't look happy.

In the afternoon, we rode the ferry out to the islands we saw from the CN Tower. There aren't any cars there. We rented bikes and rode along the boardwalks. Rachel picked up a few rocks from the beach to add to her collection. We saw the squirrels we couldn't see from the top of the tower, and forgot for a while that we were even in a big city.

Exceedingly Weird

Don't forget to look up when you walk along the streets in Toronto. We found this car bursting out of a building on Queen Street. Its wheels were spinning, so it looks as if it has just come crashing through the wall. We also saw half a cow sticking out of a building on King Street. That must have hurt!

Getting around by streetcar

This is looking waaaaay up.

This is looking waaaaay down.

59

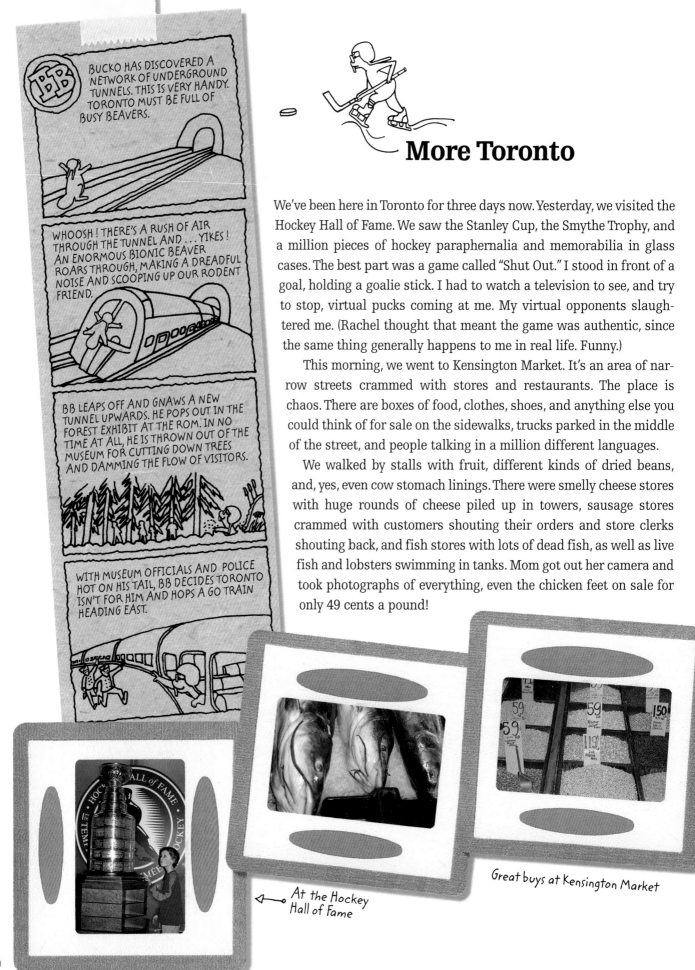

BUCKO HAS DISCOVERED A NETWORK OF UNDERGROUND TUNNELS. THIS IS VERY HANDY. TORONTO MUST BE FULL OF BUSY BEAVERS.

WHOOSH! THERE'S A RUSH OF AIR THROUGH THE TUNNEL AND ... YIKES! AN ENORMOUS BIONIC BEAVER ROARS THROUGH, MAKING A DREADFUL NOISE AND SCOOPING UP OUR RODENT FRIEND.

BB LEAPS OFF AND GNAWS A NEW TUNNEL UPWARDS. HE POPS OUT IN THE FOREST EXHIBIT AT THE ROM. IN NO TIME AT ALL, HE IS THROWN OUT OF THE MUSEUM FOR CUTTING DOWN TREES AND DAMMING THE FLOW OF VISITORS.

WITH MUSEUM OFFICIALS AND POLICE HOT ON HIS TAIL, BB DECIDES TORONTO ISN'T FOR HIM AND HOPS A GO TRAIN HEADING EAST.

More Toronto

We've been here in Toronto for three days now. Yesterday, we visited the Hockey Hall of Fame. We saw the Stanley Cup, the Smythe Trophy, and a million pieces of hockey paraphernalia and memorabilia in glass cases. The best part was a game called "Shut Out." I stood in front of a goal, holding a goalie stick. I had to watch a television to see, and try to stop, virtual pucks coming at me. My virtual opponents slaughtered me. (Rachel thought that meant the game was authentic, since the same thing generally happens to me in real life. Funny.)

This morning, we went to Kensington Market. It's an area of narrow streets crammed with stores and restaurants. The place is chaos. There are boxes of food, clothes, shoes, and anything else you could think of for sale on the sidewalks, trucks parked in the middle of the street, and people talking in a million different languages.

We walked by stalls with fruit, different kinds of dried beans, and, yes, even cow stomach linings. There were smelly cheese stores with huge rounds of cheese piled up in towers, sausage stores crammed with customers shouting their orders and store clerks shouting back, and fish stores with lots of dead fish, as well as live fish and lobsters swimming in tanks. Mom got out her camera and took photographs of everything, even the chicken feet on sale for only 49 cents a pound!

← At the Hockey Hall of Fame

Great buys at Kensington Market

We made our way along Spadina Avenue through one of Toronto's four Chinatowns. Suddenly, we were on Queen Street West. A whole new world! Make that another planet. We sat on a bench to rest and watch the people go by. It seems as if to be on Queen Street you have to wear funky fashions and hairstyles. We saw someone with huge platform heels and purple hair. I decided I'm going to set my first science fiction movie on Queen Street.

We finished off the day at the Royal Ontario Museum, also known as the ROM. There was lots of stuff to look at, like cool jewels and gemstones and huge dinosaur skeletons. The partially unwrapped mummy in the Egyptian section, with his toes sticking out, gave Rachel the creeps. But even she liked walking through the replica of a bat cave. Our favourite place in the museum was the special room for kids. We got to use microscopes and touch lots of artifacts, like chain mail and fossils.

Food I Was Introduced to for My Own Good

Mom and Dad suggested we stop in Chinatown for some dim sum for lunch. Rachel and I suggested we have sum thing else, like hot dogs, but they didn't seem to hear us. The restaurant was packed with people, and the servers wheeled the food around on carts, calling out the names of all kinds of food I didn't recognize. I did recognize the chicken feet, after our introduction to them this morning. The food comes in small servings, so the point seems to be to try many different dishes. I filled up on spring rolls, but I think everyone else, even Rachel, tried one of everything that came by.

Cow's stomach linings. Really and truly!

Good news for me! There's a lot more to multiculturalism than trying new foods. Our taxi driver told us about Caribana, a gigantic Caribbean parade and celebration held each August in Toronto. Lots of music, dancing, and colourful costumes! It sounds great.

Niagara Escarpment explained
at the Welland Centre

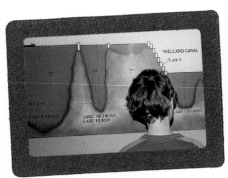

Lake levels also explained

Stylish moose hat
from the gift shop

According to Dad

The falls are on the move!
Twelve thousand years ago
they were 11 km (7 miles)
downstream from where
they are today.

The tumbling water keeps
eroding the cliff edge,
causing large sections of
rock to fall away. The
falls used to move about
a metre (3 ft.) upstream
each year, but now they
have slowed down to just
a few centimtres/inches
a year. Still, in a millen-
nium or so, someone will
have to move all those
tourist shops upstream.

From: gbowers@galaxy.com
Subject: The BIG Splooosh!

Hey Kyle!

Today we saw Niagara Falls from above, from behind, and even from a boat at the base of the falls. So many exciting ways to get soaked!

The falls look just like that photo in our social studies textbook. In fact, I kept thinking maybe I was looking at that photo, except for the thundering sound of crashing water and the fact that I spent the day soaking wet.

There are really two sets of falls, the Canadian Falls and the American Falls. The Canadian Falls are bigger (this must annoy the Americans) and curve in a horseshoe shape. Niagara Falls also has the largest concentration of gift shops and tacky Canadian souvenirs you ever saw. Don't worry, I didn't forget about you when I was in the gift shop.

There are lots of stories of people going over the falls. A seven-year-old boy from Tennessee fell out of a boat upstream of Niagara Falls and went over without even breaking a bone. Various other wackos have gone over on purpose—in barrels, diving bells, kayaks (not recommended), parachutes that failed to open (ditto), and other containers. Some didn't live to tell about it. What's more surprising is that some did.

We spent the afternoon watching freighters go through the locks on the Welland Canal. Ships can travel all the way through the Great Lakes, but between Lake Ontario and Lake Erie it gets tricky. That's where Niagara Falls is. The freighters can bypass the falls, but they still have to get over that darned cliff called the Niagara Escarpment. To do this, they "climb" almost 100 m (330 ft.) through the canal's eight locks. That makes the Welland Canal the tallest water staircase in the world. It's one of the world's greatest engi-neering feats, according to our brochure.

We're going to Ottawa tomorrow. I'll say hi to the prime minister for you.

Later, Guy

Niagara Falls

Ottawa

We've made it to Ottawa, the nation's capital. On our first day we toured the Parliament Buildings. They are very fancy. The best room was the library. Flowers, masks, and mythical creatures are carved into the wood in the room and the provincial and territorial coats of arms are on the walls. Somebody put a lot of work into that room.

We also got a peek at what goes on inside these buildings. After lunch we went into the public gallery and watched Question Period. The politicians yelled, cheered, and booed at each other, and thumped their desks while people were speaking. If my class at school behaved like that, we would be in big trouble!

The Speaker wears a strange hat and sits on a big chair. I would have thought people would make fun of his hat, but they don't. Each day that Parliament is sitting, the Speaker carries the mace into the House of Commons. The mace is ceremonial and symbolic. It's supposed to remind all politicians that the Speaker has legislative authority and can throw them out if they don't behave. The Speaker probably never actually bops anyone with it. The funny thing is, when politicians want to say something to each other, they say it to the Speaker instead.

Yawn

Rachel and I had a mock Question Period of our own. It went like this:

Guy: Mr. Speaker, I would like to bring your attention to an outrageous situation. Rachel got more ice cream than I did for dessert!

Mom (standing in as the Members of Parliament on my team): Yes! Not fair! Boo!

Rachel: Mr. Speaker, the honourable member opposite has rocks in his head. He had way more ice cream than I did!

Dad (representing the Members of Parliament on Rachel's side): Boo! He's a liar!

The Canadian Museum of Nature

The Canada Aviation Museum

The Canada Agriculture Museum

The Canadian Centre for Caricature

The Canadian Museum of Contemporary Photography

The Canadian Ski Museum

The Royal Canadian Mint

The Currency Museum

Maybe next time...

There are lots of museums in Ottawa! Yesterday we visited the Canada Science and Technology Museum. Dad and I took a motion-simulated virtual visit to Mars, zooming through asteroids and crash-landing. It was amazing! I also tried steering a model ship through a channel full of icebergs. Rachel operated a model Canadarm. She couldn't get it to scratch her back, which would have been useful.

We spent the evening at the Museum of Civilization in Gatineau. Luckily they have high ceilings, because the totem poles there are tall! I liked the Canada Hall. When we walked through the exhibits, we felt like we were reliving the history of Canada. We finished up by going to the IMAX movie theatre.

Today, it was the Canadian War Museum. A tour guide took us through the exhibits, telling us the behind-the-scenes information about Canada's role in various wars. We walked through replicas of First World War trenches with sandbags, barbed wire, and even rats. We also went inside a simulator to experience what it was like for Second World War Canadian troops landing on the beaches of Normandy, France, on D-Day. We also learned about some tragic war campaigns, such as those at Dieppe and in Hong Kong, where many Canadians died. It sure made you think, and we were all pretty quiet when we came out of the War Museum into the bright sunshine. Even Rachel was silent. For exactly 3 minutes and 35 seconds.

According to Mom

We bicycled along the Rideau Canal. It's 200 km (124 miles) long, so we didn't see the whole thing. Mom told us it links the Ottawa River at Ottawa with Lake Ontario at Kingston. The canal was built by hand by British troops and many Irish labourers in 1826–32. In their on-going feuds with the Americans, the British wanted the canal to be their sneaky alternative route from Ottawa to Lake Ontario in case the Americans prevented them from going up the St. Lawrence. Now the Rideau Canal is the world's longest skating rink.

Hand stamp at the Museum of Science and Technology

At the Museum of Civilization

Great satellite at the Museum of Science and Technology

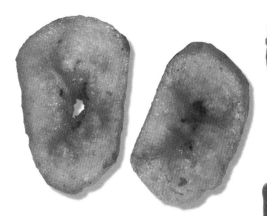

Cheerio, Ontario!

Ontario is big, but we managed to see and do a lot.

We did have to promise Dad that next time we'd go to Point Pelee National Park. He's very disappointed we missed it. It's a bird-watcher's paradise. He wants to come back in May when the warblers migrate through. He thinks it will be fun to get up at dawn to hear all the birds sing. I don't, but I would like to be able to say I've been to Point Pelee. It's the southernmost tip of Canada's mainland (on the same latitude as Rome, Italy, and northern California!).

Things We'll Do and Places We'll Go Next Time

1. Go canoeing in Algonquin Park, and whitewater rafting through the rapids of the Ottawa or Mattawa rivers.

2. Mom, Dad, and Rachel want to hike along the Bruce Trail. (Not me. I don't hike.)

3. Take the Polar Bear Express (it's a train) from Cochrane to Moosonee. Find out if they make moose at Moose Factory.

4. Go down into the underground gold mine in Timmins.

According to Dad

There's the Tulip Festival in Ottawa every May. Queen Juliana of the Netherlands was allowed to stay in Canada to be safe during the Second World War. The Netherlands is famous for its tulips, and to say thank you to Canadians for their hospitality, Queen Juliana sent 10,000 bulbs to Ottawa. The royal family and tulip producers in the Netherlands continue to send bulbs each year.

Exceedingly Weird

Ottawa specializes in statues. There's one of Samuel de Champlain standing in a hero pose overlooking the Ottawa River. Champlain explored the Ottawa River by canoe in 1613. He is holding up an astrolabe, which Dad says was used to figure out where the heck they were. So Champlain probably thinks he's lost. (The explorers usually were.) He might stay lost, too. We found out that he's holding the astrolabe upside down!

Indigo bunting

Scarlet tanager

Cape May warbler

Met this big guy at the Welland Canals Centre. He's a Mohawk lacrosse player. Lacrosse is Canada's oldest organized sport. The Algonquians and Iroquoians were playing it long before the French and British came along.

5. In Toronto, visit the Ontario Science Centre. And then get to Sudbury and visit Science North.

6. Visit Ottawa during Winterlude in February to see the ice sculptures and to skate on the Rideau Canal.

7. See the street performers at the Kingston Buskers Rendezvous.

8. Take a boat trip through the 47 locks on the Rideau Canal.

9. Visit more museums in Ottawa.

(Hey—who added that to the list? Mom!)

René's Cat Village, Ottawa, Ontario

Dear Brittany:
Guess what we found in the trees behind the Parliament Buildings? A home for stray cats! (One of the cats is called Fluffy!) They live in little wooden houses, with straw beds. A man called René feeds them and cleans their cat village every day. He feeds wild pigeons, raccoons, and squirrels, too. He showed us how he has taught a squirrel to take peanuts from his ear.
Your friend,
(Guess!)

CANADA

CANADA 5
Ontario · Ontario
Wine Route

René's Cat Village

Finally, scenery interesting to Fluffy.

Dictionnaire Rodent-Français

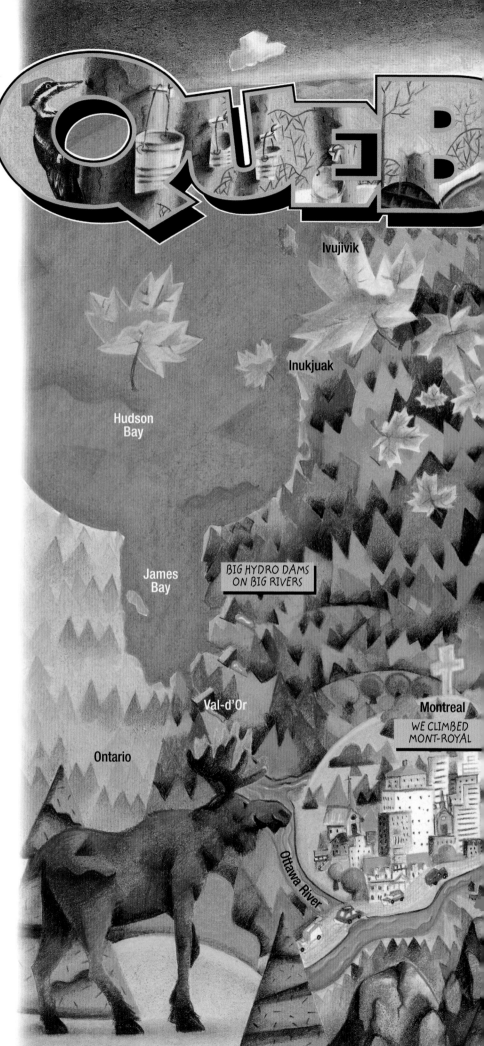

QUEB

Ivujivik

Inukjuak

Hudson Bay

James Bay

BIG HYDRO DAMS ON BIG RIVERS

Val-d'Or

Montreal

WE CLIMBED MONT-ROYAL

Ontario

Ottawa River

We have reached Quebec—the largest province in Canada. It's known as "la belle province." French and English are the official languages of Canada. Most people who live in Quebec speak French, so Rachel and I have a chance to use the French we have been learning at school. I'm suddenly wishing I had paid much more attention.

It turns out Mom speaks some French that she learned in those dark ages B.C. ("Before Children"). Dad, on the other hand, thinks he can speak French but doesn't realize that no one can understand his accent. Rachel, of course, can sing "Alouette" in French. Unfortunately. All I need to remember is that I can find my way out of most tricky situations by looking for a sign that says "Sortie."

Provincial Flag

Provincial Flower Blue Flag

Provincial Arms

Ungava
Bay

Labrador

Blanc Sablon

Harrington
Harbour

Chibougamou

Natashquan

ROAD ENDS
TAKE FREIGHTER

Sept-Îles

Labrador Current

COLD TAP

Isle d'Anticosti

Saguenay River

Chicoutimi

Gulf of St. Lawrence

Laurentides

Forillon National Park

GOOD SKIPPING
STONES

Gaspésie

St. Lawrence Seaway

Trois-
Rivières

Quebec City

Rocher Percé

A HOLE IN ONE!

PLAINS OF
ABRAHAM

MANY MESSY
SEABIRDS

Tropical Current

HOT TAP

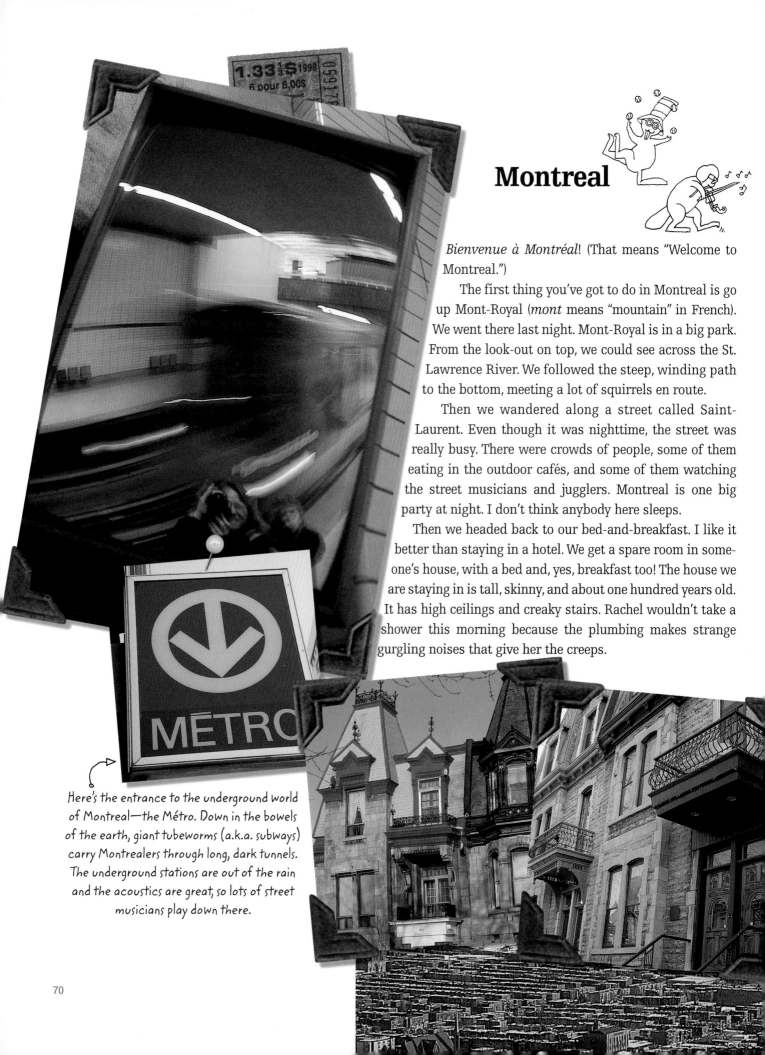

Montreal

Bienvenue à Montréal! (That means "Welcome to Montreal.")

The first thing you've got to do in Montreal is go up Mont-Royal (*mont* means "mountain" in French). We went there last night. Mont-Royal is in a big park. From the look-out on top, we could see across the St. Lawrence River. We followed the steep, winding path to the bottom, meeting a lot of squirrels en route.

Then we wandered along a street called Saint-Laurent. Even though it was nighttime, the street was really busy. There were crowds of people, some of them eating in the outdoor cafés, and some of them watching the street musicians and jugglers. Montreal is one big party at night. I don't think anybody here sleeps.

Then we headed back to our bed-and-breakfast. I like it better than staying in a hotel. We get a spare room in someone's house, with a bed and, yes, breakfast too! The house we are staying in is tall, skinny, and about one hundred years old. It has high ceilings and creaky stairs. Rachel wouldn't take a shower this morning because the plumbing makes strange gurgling noises that give her the creeps.

Here's the entrance to the underground world of Montreal—the Métro. Down in the bowels of the earth, giant tubeworms (a.k.a. subways) carry Montrealers through long, dark tunnels. The underground stations are out of the rain and the acoustics are great, so lots of street musicians play down there.

On that theme, today's sight-seeing started at a graveyard in the centre of Montreal. Or, as Dad said, the *dead* centre.

"Old joke," I said.

"Old graveyard," said Mom.

It's in the Pointe-à-Callière Museum of Archeology and History in Vieux Montréal (Old Montreal). The museum is built around an archeological dig of early Montreal, which includes an old cemetery. Spooky!

Different people have occupied this very spot for centuries, starting with the Iroquois people long before the French settled here. Over the years, one thing was built on top of another. So if you dig down, right underneath the present-day streets of Montreal, you can uncover layers of evidence of settlements, like old graveyards, from different times long ago.

Afterwards, we wandered along the cobblestone streets of Old Montreal for a while, looking at old things. When Mom saw we were starting to overdose on history and collapse from exhaustion, she led us into an old stone building. Surprise! We were in the Café Électronique. Rachel and I played computer games while Mom and Dad drank café au lait.

According to Mom

Montreal is Canada's second-biggest city and the world's second-largest French-speaking city (after Paris, France). We heard lots of different languages being spoken as we wandered around. Mom said that people here don't just speak English and French. There are Montrealers who speak Yiddish, Italian, Portuguese, Chinese, Greek, Haitian, Jamaican, Vietnamese, and all sorts of other languages.

Exceedingly Weird

There are people here who tie themselves up in knots and fly through the air with nothing holding them! They're in an amazing circus called the Cirque du Soleil (that means the Circus of the Sun in English). It's based in Montreal but travels all over the world. It includes contortionists who can twist themselves into all kinds of crazy pretzel shapes and high-flying acrobats who give me the shivers watching what they do up there. It's great to see, but I think I'll just stay on solid ground and watch.

71

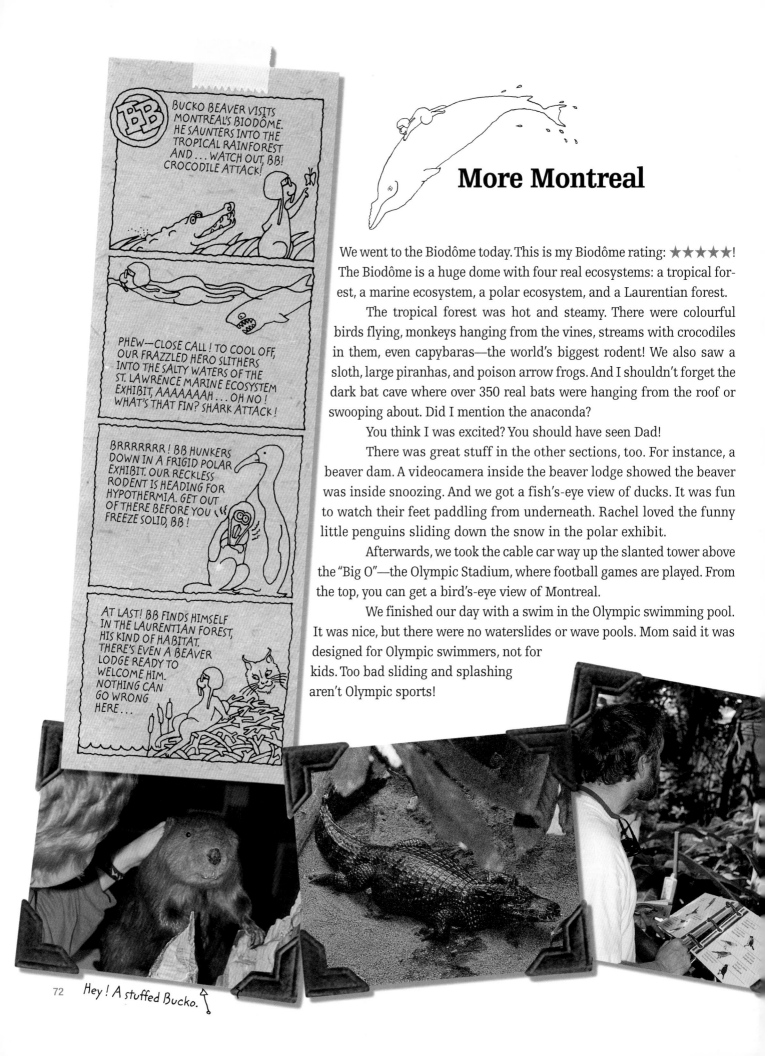

Comic strip (left margin)

Panel 1: BUCKO BEAVER VISITS MONTREAL'S BIODÔME. HE SAUNTERS INTO THE TROPICAL RAINFOREST AND...WATCH OUT, BB! CROCODILE ATTACK!

Panel 2: PHEW—CLOSE CALL! TO COOL OFF, OUR FRAZZLED HERO SLITHERS INTO THE SALTY WATERS OF THE ST. LAWRENCE MARINE ECOSYSTEM EXHIBIT, AAAAAAAH...OH NO! WHAT'S THAT FIN? SHARK ATTACK!

Panel 3: BRRRRRRR! BB HUNKERS DOWN IN A FRIGID POLAR EXHIBIT. OUR RECKLESS RODENT IS HEADING FOR HYPOTHERMIA. GET OUT OF THERE BEFORE YOU FREEZE SOLID, BB!

Panel 4: AT LAST! BB FINDS HIMSELF IN THE LAURENTIAN FOREST, HIS KIND OF HABITAT. THERE'S EVEN A BEAVER LODGE READY TO WELCOME HIM. NOTHING CAN GO WRONG HERE...

More Montreal

We went to the Biodôme today. This is my Biodôme rating: ★★★★★! The Biodôme is a huge dome with four real ecosystems: a tropical forest, a marine ecosystem, a polar ecosystem, and a Laurentian forest.

The tropical forest was hot and steamy. There were colourful birds flying, monkeys hanging from the vines, streams with crocodiles in them, even capybaras—the world's biggest rodent! We also saw a sloth, large piranhas, and poison arrow frogs. And I shouldn't forget the dark bat cave where over 350 real bats were hanging from the roof or swooping about. Did I mention the anaconda?

You think I was excited? You should have seen Dad!

There was great stuff in the other sections, too. For instance, a beaver dam. A videocamera inside the beaver lodge showed the beaver was inside snoozing. And we got a fish's-eye view of ducks. It was fun to watch their feet paddling from underneath. Rachel loved the funny little penguins sliding down the snow in the polar exhibit.

Afterwards, we took the cable car way up the slanted tower above the "Big O"—the Olympic Stadium, where football games are played. From the top, you can get a bird's-eye view of Montreal.

We finished our day with a swim in the Olympic swimming pool. It was nice, but there were no waterslides or wave pools. Mom said it was designed for Olympic swimmers, not for kids. Too bad sliding and splashing aren't Olympic sports!

Hey! A stuffed Bucko.

Guy's Wildlife List
Capybara

According to Dad

The Biodôme had a special exhibit on belugas while we were there. Belugas are those white whales that make all kinds of squawking and whistling noises and always look like they're smiling. Most live in the Arctic, but there are some in the St. Lawrence River. Those belugas are in big trouble, though, because of the pollution in the river. It's very sad. It's scary, too. If belugas are in trouble, what about us? The Earth is our habitat, too.

The Plains of Abraham

Battlefields Park

Quebec City

We drove along the St. Lawrence River from Montreal yesterday. Now we are in Quebec City (not to be confused with the province of Quebec, where we also are), the only walled city in North America.

Today we found out that battles are a specialty of Quebec City. We began the day by going to a museum called Musée du Fort. There is a huge model diorama here that shows Quebec City as it would have appeared around 1750, and it's used to re-enact some of the battles that were fought in Quebec.

We saw on a map how Quebec is situated at the "bottleneck" of the St. Lawrence River, right where the river starts to get skinny. (Turns out the word "Quebec" comes from a word in the Algonquin language. *Quebecq* means "the river narrows here." Which it does.) The Algonquins are Native people who lived in this area before the French or English did.

In the scramble for new land, especially between the English and the French, this area was very important. Since the river was the handiest route into the interior of North America, everybody wanted control of the bottleneck area. Then you could block everybody else from getting into North America.

According to Mom

Mom gave a brief overview of the many battles that were fought over Quebec. First, the Iroquois were here. Then, in 1608 the French explorer Samuel de Champlain established a fur post here that became the capital of France's North American territories (New France). Then the English swiped it, then the French got it back, but the English kept attacking.

It got really tense in 1759 when the British, under General Wolfe, sneaked up the cliffs near Quebec City in the dark of night onto the Plains of Abraham. The French, under their leader, Montcalm, marched to meet the British forces. But the French lost the battle. In fact, that was the battle that pretty well finished New France. Wolfe and Montcalm died heroically, and the British got control of the bottleneck. That meant that, later, they had to deal with attacking Americans.

In Quebec City there are lots of flower gardens planted to make words or pictures. This one's a fleur-de-lis, the unofficial emblem of Quebec.

In comparison, life is pretty quiet in Quebec City these days. Now the old cannons and mortars used to protect the city are mostly used for kids to climb on. There are lots of them on the old wall that surrounds the high part of the old city. From there you can look down onto enemy intruders. It would be fun to have a cannon, but Mom said they're too heavy to bring home as souvenirs. (She has no appreciation of history.)

We also went to Battlefields Park. Inside, in Joan of Arc Park, back in 1880, it's believed our national anthem, *O Canada,* was played for the first time. In the centre of the park are the Plains of Abraham, where there was a major battle between the British and French in 1759.

✦CANADA✦

Dear Brittany:
We're in Quebec City. It's old. I mean really, really old. It looks like a storybook town, with narrow cobblestone streets surrounded by an old rock wall. We may be able to go on a horse-and-wagon ride through the city this afternoon!
I'm learning more French. I already know to go into "Dames" and not "Hommes."
Salut! Rachel

CANADA

Streets of Vieux Quebec, Quebec City

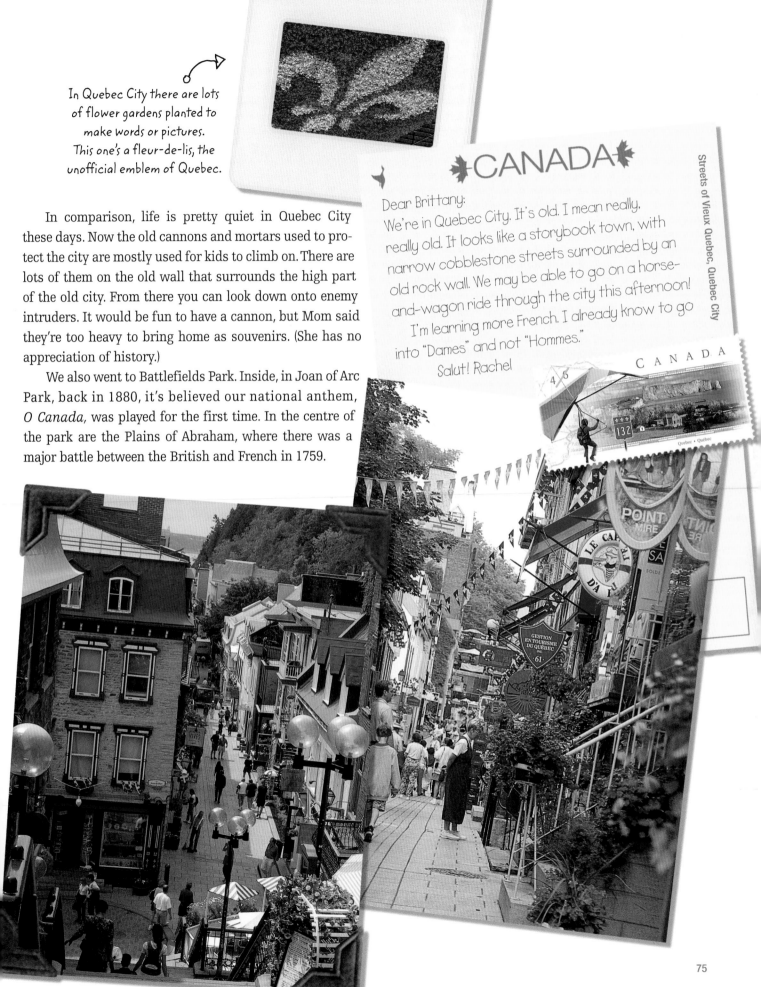

According to Dad

The Gulf of St. Lawrence is one of the most difficult waterways to navigate in the world. There's fog, wind, strong currents, winter ice, and treacherous reefs just under the surface of the water. There are even icebergs. Sometimes ships have to manoeuver through a narrow channel to avoid submerged rocks. If a ship is a little bit off-course, it can end in disaster. Ship captains use two buoy markers on shore to position the ship exactly in the channel. They steer directly toward the buoy markers, so that one appears directly behind the other. If the ship goes even a little off-course, it's easy to tell because the buoys appear to be moving apart sideways.

The North Shore

We're driving east along the north shore of the St. Lawrence, through a hilly region called Charlevoix. Mom's oohing and aahing at the scenery, and is about to wring my neck for having my nose inside a book. Rachel's singing "Alouette." Dad has that look on his face like he's trying to pretend he can't hear anything and none of us is here.

Rachel stops singing long enough to say, "A lot of the houses have those funny-shaped roofs."

Mom says they're called mansard roofs.

"What's an *auberge*?" Dad asks, rejoining us on planet earth. "I've seen lots of signs for them."

"It sounds familiar, but I can't remember. Rachel, could you check the dictionary?" asks Mom.

"It's an eggplant."

"An eggplant? Rachel, it can't be! May I see the dictionary?" Mom asked. "Aha! An *auberge* is an inn. Eggplant is *aubergine*. Close, but different."

"I guess," says Rachel, and starts singing again.

Guy's Wildlife List
Dinosaur

I found these dinosaurs roaming around the wharf at Ragueneau. It must be a very rare sighting, because dinosaurs aren't even listed in our wildlife guidebook for this area!

Loading a car on the freighter

Later, we ran out of road, so now we're on a freighter. Our car is in a big container that was lifted by the ship's crane onto the deck. There are lots more containers piled on top. We hope our car isn't squished.

We have a tiny cabin crammed with four bunks. We go to sleep feeling the sway of the ship and the engine vibrations. The swaying makes Rachel queasy. Dad says the reason people get seasick is because the brain gets confused between what it sees and what it feels. The trick is to look at the horizon, not something on the boat, so that you see the horizon moving up and down at the same time you feel the motion. Oddly enough, it works.

This freighter stops at little fishing ports that can't be reached by road, dropping off supplies and locals coming back from shopping or dentist appointments in the city. Some are French-speaking communities, some are English-speaking, and some are Native Montagnais villages, where residents speak their traditional language. We've met lots of interesting people. Passengers on the freighter include locals, tourists like us along for the cruise, and a few kayakers who want to be dropped off up the coast.

This is Harrington Harbour, my favourite village on the North Shore. Only a few hundred people live here. All over the rocky cove they've built funky, higgledy-piggledy boardwalks and bridges linking the wooden houses. The villagers ride all-terrain vehicles (ATVs) in the summer and snowmobiles in the winter. Instead of cars, boats are moored in front of the houses.

We camped at Forillon National Park. The pebbles on the beach were rounded and flat—perfect skipping stones.

On the Gaspé, there are signs warning that waves can wash over the road.

Gasp. Gasp.

Gaspésie

We are on the (shudder, gasp!) Gaspé Peninsula. It's believed that its name comes from the Native word *gaspeg*, meaning "where the world ends." People here call it Gaspésie. On a map, it's the tongue that sticks out of the mouth of the St. Lawrence River and into the Atlantic Ocean. Of course, we've driven all the way to the tip of the tongue, along the winding highway along the wiggly coastline. The views were amazing! We drove up over hills and down into pebbly coves lined with white-painted villages. Each one had a church spire. Rachel found some spires more "inspiring" than others. (That's her joke, not mine.)

After several days of driving and many pillow fights in the backseat, we finally arrived at Rocher Percé (which means "pierced rock"). It is a huge, 5-million-tonne chunk of rock just offshore that has a hole pierced (*percé*) through the middle.

We took a great boat trip out around the rock and then to Île Bonaventure, an island offshore. There is a bird sanctuary on the island. The birds nest on narrow ledges on huge vertical cliffs that rise straight out of the water. Imagine cruising by on a boat and smelling a cliff plastered with droppings from thousands of fish-eating birds. Pheeeeeeew! Mostly we saw big white gannets that can dive-bomb vertically into the water to snatch fish. There were also gulls called kittiwakes and murres, which look like mini-penguins. They were all swooping around in a huge screeching and squawking blizzard.

We landed on the island, and Rachel and I poked about on the beach. Dad hiked around the island for a closer look at the colony. He said that, close up, the stink was truly indescribable. (Use your imagination.)

Our campsite tonight looks out over Rocher Percé. Mom plans on taking the perfect sunset photo. Once again. . .

Rocher Percé—a hole in one!

Mom's perfect sunset shot

Guy's Wildlife List
Gannets

EXCURSION
ÎLE BONAVENTURE
6$/pers. taxes incluses

By boat to the bird sanctuary
on Île Bonaventure

79

Look, a human!

Au Revoir, Quebec

Whale-watching at Pointe Noire.

Our French has definitely improved, and we're moving on. Mom reminded us we can keep using it because French doesn't stop at the Quebec border. It's the Maritimes next. *À bientôt, la belle province!*

Things We'll Do and Places We'll Go Next Time

1. In Montreal, we'll go skating in the summertime at the ice rink at l'Amphitheatre Bell. And Mom wants to visit Saint-Joseph's Oratory.

2. Visit the Eastern Townships, outside of Montreal. In the spring, we can watch the "sugaring-off," when sap is collected from the maple trees and boiled down until it is syrup.

3. We'll take a boat up the Saguenay River and visit Lac-Saint-Jean.

4. Go farther north and explore some of Quebec's parks in the Laurentians, such as Parc de Mont-Tremblant and La Mauricie. Also Parc du Mont-Sainte-Anne, where I can cheat and take the cable car to the top of the "Mont."

5. Go boating around the islands of Mingan Archipelago National Park Reserve (near Havre-Saint-Pierre). We'll see funny-shaped rocks and funny-looking puffins.

Food I Was Introduced to for My Own Good

Mom decided it was time we tried poutine. Poutine is a Quebec favourite. It's not just french fries. It's not even just french fries with gravy. It's french fries with gravy with cheese curds. You can buy it in the little fast-food take-out places (called *casse-croûte*) that are everywhere in Quebec. So we screeched to a halt in front of Doreen's Casse-Croûte for some real, gooey poutine.

6. Go to Cap-Tourmente National Wildlife Area or the islands off Montmagny (on the Gaspé) in the spring or fall to see the snow geese migration.

7. Go to Saint-Louis-du-Ha!Ha!, on the Gaspé, just so we can tell our friends we did.

8. I want to come back and ride "The Monster" roller coaster at La Ronde, the huge amusement park in Montreal.

9. We'll visit a salmon-viewing centre on the Matane River. There's a glass window where you can see under water and watch Atlantic salmon swimming up the spawning ladder.

10. We'll come to Quebec City during the Winter Carnival to see ice-sculpting and say hello to Bonhomme, the snowman!

According to Mom

Whales hang out where the Saguenay River flows into the St. Lawrence River. There's deep water there and lots of food (whales adore shrimp and capelin). You can watch them from the Pointe Noire Coastal Station on the south side of the Saguenay River or from the Marine Mammal Interpretive Centre in Tadoussac.

Scientists are doing studies to see if all the whale-watching cruises that are so popular now are disrupting the whales' natural behaviour. (If you had boats circling you and hundreds of tourists ogling you, would that change your behaviour?)

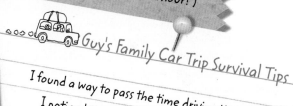

Guy's Family Car Trip Survival Tips

I found a way to pass the time driving through Quebec. I noticed that there are a lot of places that start with "Saint" in Quebec. Check out the map. The alphabetical index to our Quebec road map has a special section just for names that begin with "Saint." I counted them. It's ten times as long as the regular "S" section!

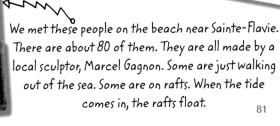

We met these people on the beach near Sainte-Flavie. There are about 80 of them. They are all made by a local sculptor, Marcel Gagnon. Some are just walking out of the sea. Some are on rafts. When the tide comes in, the rafts float.

CAMPFIRE CHAT

Ici on parle français

"Dessert time!" said Rachel, jumping up from her seat by the campfire. "Where are the donuts?"

"What donuts?" asked Mom.

"We bought some Quebec donuts today while you were grocery shopping," I said.

"Just in case you forgot to buy some," explained Dad.

"Smart thinking," said Mom.

"But it wasn't easy," said Rachel, "because our designated French-speaker wasn't with us. Only Dad was. And he isn't."

"Uh oh. What happened?" asked Mom.

"*Pas de problemo!*" said Dad. "I just pointed to the donuts we wanted."

"Except we have no idea what's inside them," I said. "I think we ended up with too many jelly ones."

"Dad tried using his *beaucoup* terrible franglais," said Rachel.

"A desperate move on my part," admitted Dad. "Fortunately, Guy remembered a few crucial words and saved the day. Pass me a donut, please, Rachel."

As we were munching, Rachel said, "On the other hand, all the people we met in Harrington Harbour spoke English."

"That's right," said Mom. "There are English-speaking villages in Quebec along the North Shore. In the Gaspé, too."

"Before we came, I thought all Quebec was French-speaking," I said.

"Mostly it is, but there are anglophones in Quebec. Just like there are francophones in Ontario, New Brunswick, and most other provinces."

"And telephones in B.C.," said Dad.

"So, how do I ever know which language to learn to speak?" asked Rachel.

"Maybe you should learn both," said Mom.

"Particularly if you like donuts," said Dad.

"Which are actually called *beignes* in French," said Mom.

"Since there are more English-speakers," said Rachel, "why don't French-speaking people just learn English?"

"Spoken like a true anglophone," said Mom. "Well, because their French language is part of who they are. They don't want to lose their francophone identity. They want to keep the language and culture alive. That's why there are laws in Quebec about using French on store signs, for example. Besides, all Canadians, not just those in Quebec, benefit from the richness of having a bilingual country."

"Must be bedtime," said Dad.

"You always think it's time for bed!" I told him.

"It always is!" said Dad.

"*Bonne nuit,*" said Mom.

"*Bonne nuit,*" said Rachel and I back.

I'm Bud the Spud.

Charming.

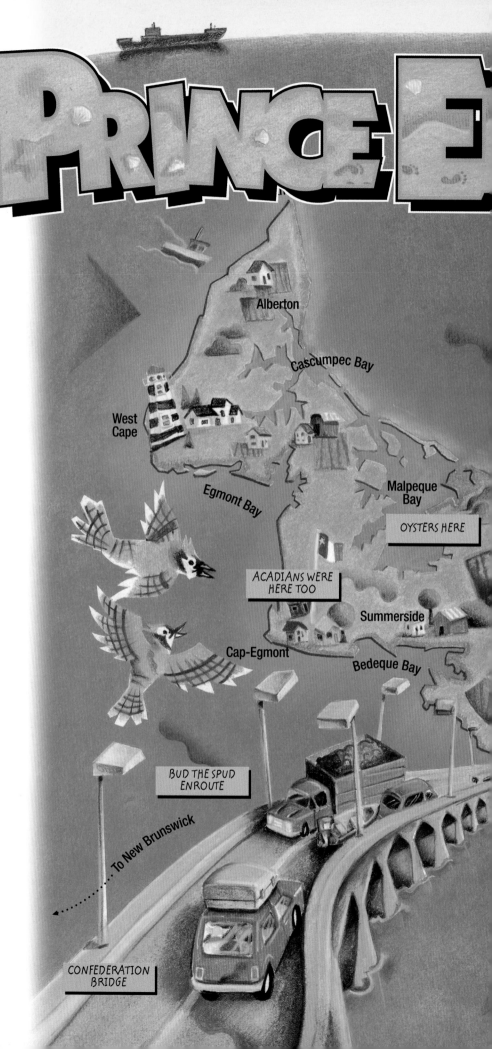

Alberton

Cascumpec Bay

West Cape

Egmont Bay

Malpeque Bay

OYSTERS HERE

ACADIANS WERE HERE TOO

Summerside

Cap-Egmont

Bedeque Bay

BUD THE SPUD ENROUTE

To New Brunswick

CONFEDERATION BRIDGE

We've conquered one of the longest bridges in the world—the almost 13 km (8 mile) long Confederation Bridge, from New Brunswick to Prince Edward Island. The bridge is so long they had to build a curve into it so drivers wouldn't fall asleep. It would be a really bad idea to fall asleep while driving on a concrete strip 40 m (130 ft.) above the water.

Mom's guidebook says PEI is the most densely populated province in Canada. That doesn't mean there are lots more people than anywhere else—it means there aren't as many places to put them, since PEI is a small province. You can drive anywhere in a couple of hours.

Provincial Arms

Provincial Flower
Lady's Slipper

Provincial Flag

WARD ISLAND

WARM OCEAN
CURRENTS

Gulf of St. Lawrence

East
Cape

Souris

Prince Edward Island National Park

GREEN GABLES

Charlottetown

WHERE THEY GAVE
BIRTH TO CANADA

Boughton
Bay

HOME OF BUD
THE SPUD

Georgetown
Harbour

Borden

Hillsborough Bay

Wood
Islands

Northumberland Strait

Charlottetown, Red Mud, and Spuds

We were in Charlottetown today—the capital of PEI. It's "The Birthplace of Confederation." I was afraid that meant we were in for a boring history lesson, but I was wrong. We visited Province House National Historic Site (it's awfully big for a "house") and saw a fancy room with a big table. Here, in 1864, the Fathers of Confederation first came up with the ambitious scheme that turned into this country called Canada.

Apparently, their original idea was for the three Maritime colonies—New Brunswick, Nova Scotia, and PEI—to join together so they would be strong enough to stand up to attacking Americans. But you know how it is sometimes when guys get together and talk. The ideas can get bigger and bigger. Not to mention, the men had a party with lots of champagne. In the end, the fathers decided, what the heck, let's make a *really* big country—a nation that's the whole northern half of the continent. Three years later, they'd ironed out the details, signed the papers, and—presto!—Canada!

Now I understand why we had to travel so darned far this summer.

While the guide told us about the big meeting, Rachel and I did the scavenger hunt the guides had set up. We looked for spittoons, five-headed mouse traps, and spools of ribbon. Back in those days, men used to chew tobacco and then spit it out into big jugs called spittoons. (This was considered acceptable!) As for the mice, lots of them came looking for the straw that was used to line the carpets to keep the floors warm.

They BUILDED better than they knew? Our three-year-old cousin, Megan, uses better grammar than that!

In the hearts and minds of the delegates who assembled in this room on September 1st, 1864 was born the Dominion of Canada. Providence being their Guide, they builded better than they knew .

Here's what was written on a plaque outside the Confederation Chamber.

The red ribbon was used to tie up legal documents and make them look important.

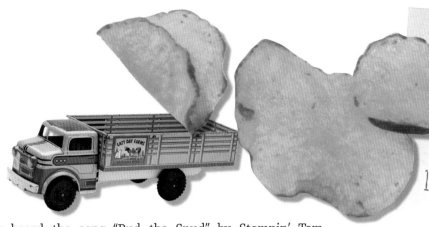

Ever heard the song "Bud the Spud" by Stompin' Tom Connors? Stompin' Tom's from PEI, so Mom bought the tape here. I've now heard it at least six times. Rachel loves that song. We've been cruising along PEI roads, my mother swooning over the scenery and threatening never to leave this place, and Rachel and Tom singing at the top of their lungs. In case you didn't know, PEI is famous for potatoes. There's even a potato museum here. (Maybe *next* time. . .) We've driven by fields and fields of potato plants. Once we passed a truck loaded with spuds, and Rachel went wild. "There's Bud the Spud!"

Food I Was Introduced to for My Own Good

We went out for a lobster dinner, because that's a PEI tradition. Grown adults wearing bibs! Dad, of course, had to explain the anatomy of the crustacean before he could eat it. No way that I was going to eat a boiled-alive lobster after that! Instead, I had my authentic PEI spuds in the shape of french fries.

Exceedingly Weird

Lobster Facts

1. Lobsters are prehistoric wonders. They haven't changed in 100 million years. (Lucky them; my mother makes me change every couple of days.)

2. According to our guidebook, a lobster is like something from a joke book. "It tastes with its feet, listens with its legs, and has teeth in its stomach (which is found just behind the head). The kidney is in the head, brain in the neck, and the bones (shell) are on the outside." Dad says this is probably stretching the truth, but it beats the description in the scientific literature.

3. A lobster can climb out of its shell anytime the shell gets too small.

4. Lobsters have two different front claws—like a fork and knife. The bigger crusher has rounded teeth for scrunching dinner, while the pointed cutter rips it apart.

5. Lobsters turn pink when they are dropped into boiling water. No, they don't scream. Uncooked lobsters are more likely a mottled greenish-black. We saw some lovely blue ones in an aquarium tank.

6. You can buy a lobster pot to take home as a souvenir for $5. Well, maybe YOU can. Mom said we couldn't.

Off We Go Again

As we left PEI, I got thinking about Canada. The way it ended up seems so . . . haphazard. I mean, my social studies reports are planned better than that. Like the way it ended up British rather than French, or American, for that matter. Or what if the Mi'kmaq and other Native people who lived here had told the Europeans that the land wasn't up for grabs, so please go away and do your "discovering" somewhere else? It would have made for a different trip across Canada!

Things We'll Do and Places We'll Go Next Time

1. We'll bicycle along the Confederation Trail.

2. Rachel wants to see the musical "Anne of Green Gables."

3. We can come to Charlottetown on July 1 for the big Canada Day celebrations.

4. There are lots of golf courses, so there must be mini-golf. . . .

5. We read about lighthouses that are open to the public. We'll go for a guided tour.

6. Dad says he really, REALLY wants to go to the PEI Potato Museum. (He's kidding, right?)

7. Mom doesn't want to leave, so I guess we'll see her when we come back.

Home of Anne of Green Gables, Cavendish, PEI

Dear Brittany:

Anne of Green Gables' house is surrounded by a golf course. I don't
recall Matthew and Marilla Cuthbert
playing golf in the book, do you?
Apart from that, Green Gables is
very pretty and looks just like it
should. Well, maybe without the
gift shop.

Do you know how many tourists
visit Green Gables? 250,000 a year!

Bye with an "e,"
Rachel

According to Dad

We are camping at the national park
on the north side of the island, near a
sand beach and sand dunes. Dad says
the reason the sand is such an unusual
red colour is that it's rusted. We
thought he was kidding, but it turns
out there's actually iron in the sand
here and that's what rusts.

My father, the sand expert, also
said that the clumps of grass on the
sand dunes here are very important.
It's marram grass, and when people
walk on marram grass, they kill it. If
it didn't hold the sand dunes together
with its roots, the sand would all blow
away. We did our part and stayed off
the grass, so the sand will still be here
the next time we come.

Green Gables

CANADA 45

BB USES SPUD REINFORCEMENTS
TO REMIND TOURISTS NOT TO
WALK ON THE MARRAM GRASS.

MARRAM GRASS

Okay, genius, what ingredient in toothpaste, ice cream,
and cough syrup is raked up from the beaches of PEI?
(Stand on your head to read the answer.)

Answer: It's a dark, purplish seaweed called Irish moss.

A: That's the last time I use toothpaste!

B: What about ice cream?

A: Well . . .

A

B

89

CHIRP
CHIRP CHIRP
CHIRP
CHIRP

We've crossed the border into New Brunswick. These Maritime provinces are making me sleepy. It's because we keep losing hours on this trip (maybe we'll find them at the end when we clean out the car).

Since the Maritime provinces are in the Atlantic time zone, people here get a head start on the rest of Canada every morning. It's dawn in eastern Canada four hours before the sun comes up in the west. This means my parents shake me out of my sleeping bag here every morning at three a.m.! (I've kept my watch on B.C. time, so I know.) This is cruel!

Provincial Arms

Provincial Flower
Purple Violet

Provincial Flag

Mt. Carleton
HIGH MOUNTAIN—
FOR THE MARITIMES

Fredericton

Saint John River

USA

Black's Harbour

Grand Manan
Island

Quebec

UNSWICK

Bay of Chaleurs

Acadian Historic
Village

CAUTION: TIME
WARP HERE

Gulf of St. Lawrence

Miramichi Bay

Kouchibouguac
National Park

Prince Edward
Island

Northumberland Strait

MAGNETIC HILL

Moncton

Tidal Bore

Confederation Bridge

Hopewell Cape

Saint John

NOT ST. JOHN'S

Nova Scotia

Bay of Fundy

A figurehead from the bow of an old ship.

The Acadian Coast

According to Mom

The Acadians have a tragic history. Until 1755, they lived in what used to be a French colony called Acadia. Acadia was an area that included the Maritime provinces and part of Quebec and New England, which is in the northern United States. The Acadians had been living there since the early 1600s. Then the British took over their territory. The British wanted the Acadians to sign a paper saying they were on Britain's side, not France's. But the Acadians didn't want to take sides. They just wanted to be left alone. So the British forced the Acadians to leave their homes and farms in Nova Scotia. They ended up scattered all over North America. Some of them came here, to this part of New Brunswick.

We had our first Atlantic storm last night, with howling winds, thunder, and buckets of rain. Mom rigged up a tarpaulin and cooked dinner underneath in the downpour. On nights like this we get packaged macaroni and cheese because everything else is too difficult to cook. Yahoo!

We were camping right beside the ocean, on the Bay of Chaleurs (the body of water between the Gaspé Peninsula and New Brunswick). *Chaleur* is a French word meaning "heat," which definitely exaggerates the temperature of the water.

Yesterday we went to the Acadian Historic Village, near Caraquet. It was easy to imagine what it must have been like living there 200 years ago. We saw horse-drawn wagons and Acadians dressed in old-fashioned clothes. Rachel tried spinning some fibres from a plant called flax into yarn to make clothing. She decided she doesn't have the patience to be an Acadian. The village was pretty and peaceful, but the Acadians sure had a tough life. I just know that from now on, whenever I complain about doing chores, Mom will say, "Just be glad you weren't an Acadian kid back then."

At the Acadian Historic Village

Today we drove to Kouchibouguac National Park. Come on, try to pronounce it (it's "koo-shee-boo-gwak"). The Mi'kmaq are Native people who live in the Maritimes. *Kouchibouguac* is a Mi'kmaq word that means "river of long tides."

We had a great time in the park. It has huge sandy beaches, with warm water that is great for swimming. Plus, there are lots of birds—including about 18,000 common terns—in Kouchibouguac. We watched the terns and wondered if they take turns when they swoop and make a tern... I mean *turn* in the air.

Watch out for monster lobsters in Shediac, the Lobster Capital of the World!

PINCER ALERT !

93

Look, Mom! No hands.

Guy: Hi tide.

Tide: High?
You ain't seen nothing, yet.
I'm a-coming in!

Saint John River Valley

According to Dad

The Bay of Fundy has the biggest tides in the world. Here's why:

1. They are caused by the gravitational pull of the moon and the sun. When the moon is new or full, it pulls with the sun and the pull is even stronger. When this double-pull happens at the same time as the moon's orbit is closest to the Earth, watch out! Mega-tide incoming!

2. The water in the bay sloshes from one end to the other like water in a bathtub. It takes about 13 hours for this sloshing water to travel to the end of the bay and back, and the incoming tide gives it a little extra push. This slosh makes a normal high tide even higher.

3. The Bay of Fundy becomes narrower and shallower at its end, forcing the water higher up its sides.

To: kheisler@relay.com
From: gbowers@galaxy.com
Subject: Guy: The Travelling Goofball

Yo Kyle,
I got your message. Sounds like you are having a cool time with that go-kart. Just don't crash it before I get home.

We've come into Saint John today. Not to be confused with St. John's, Newfoundland. We will be there eventually. But not today. Saint John is in New Brunswick. Someone should re-name one of those cities.

We went for a drive along the Saint John River Valley. Mom kept telling me to get my nose out of my book and look at the wonderful scenery. Okay, so it was wonderful. (So far I've read 16 books on this trip—during the times when the scenery wasn't so wonderful.)

Got to go—we're off to take a jet boat ride up the Reversing Falls. That's where the tide from the Bay of Fundy comes in so high and so fast it pushes the Saint John River backwards so it flows uphill. The pushing match produces big rapids and whirlpools. Yesterday we watched this happen from a park on shore. Pretty incredible. So incredible, we want to get even closer to the action. So today, we venture forth into the swirling, whirling, dangerous rapids in a high-speed jet boat. Will we survive? Will we get sucked under? Will we get wet? Will Rachel freak out? I can't wait to find out! Tune in next time for the thrilling sequel.
Later,
Guy

To: kheisler@relay.com
From: gbowers@galaxy.com
Subject: The Travelling Goofball—the sequel

Survival—affirmative. Wet—affirmative.

Fall colours in the Saint John River
Valley, New Brunswick

Dear Brittany:
There are lots of forests
to look at here in New Brunswick.
AND MORE FORESTS
AND MORE FORESTS
AND MORE FORESTS
And more...

Your long-ago, long-lost, long-
gone, longing-for-Fluffy friend,
Rachel

CANADA

Brit

20 R

Vict

Exceedingly Weird

Meet Fred's Frog! In 1885, a big
frog jumped into Fred Coleman's
boat. Fred took him home and
fed him. And fed him. Fred's
froggie got fatter and fatter.
Eventually he weighed 19 kg
(42 lbs). A formidably fat frog!
When he died, they stuffed
him and now he's in a glass
case in the York-Sunbury
Historical Museum in
Fredericton, the capital of
New Brunswick.

New Brunswick

CANADA
New Brunswick · Nouveau-Brunswick

Fiddling Around in New Brunswick

This fiddlehead:

* is the young, curled frond
  of certain fern plants
* tastes yummy
* is eaten especially in New
  Brunswick and Nova Scotia
* can be found in woods,
  riverbanks, and supermarket
  freezers

This fiddle-head:

* is a musician, specializing
  in playing the fiddle
* sounds terrific
* is listened to especially in New
  Brunswick and other eastern provinces
* can be found at the Miramichi
  Folksong Festival, which takes place
  every year

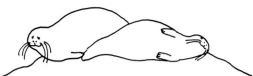

Grand Manan Island

Guy's Wildlife List
Humpback whale

"Guy, you wouldn't believe all the whales we saw this morning before you got up. It was incredible!" My parents are always telling me about things I missed because I slept in. (Only half of these things are actually true.)

As it turns out, this early morning sighting was something I really did miss. But it's okay—I got to make up for it. We went out on a whale cruise on the Bay of Fundy. The whales, mainly humpbacks, came close enough to the boat to make Rachel real nervous.

Humpbacks are big! They were surfacing and blowing balloon-shaped clouds of spray from their blowholes. Sometimes they rolled in the water and even slapped the surface with their fins. Then they dove back down, waving their tail flukes. You should have seen Dad—he was the most excited of all of us! Even our guide was pretty happy. She said we had an especially lucky day.

We're camped on Grand Manan Island, out in the middle of the Bay of Fundy. You can see the whales here, even from the shore. We all like it here—a lot. That's one of the reasons we had a family meeting. We all agreed to have a break from driving and plunk ourselves on this island for several days.

Mom says she just wants to sit on the beach with binoculars and watch for whales. And do nothing else. Not even cook. "Let them eat dulse," she says.

Food I was Introduced to for My Own Good

Dulse is a kind of seaweed we tried yesterday. People say the best dulse comes from Grand Manan Island. They collect it at low tide and dry it in the sun. Rachel actually liked it. I tried a tiny bite. Never again. No thanks. If there are no more entries in this journal after this, it's because I ate dulse and died.

Moving Right Along

We're all feeling rested and we're ready to keep on moving along. We're going to see what's on the other side of the Bay of Fundy. Hang on, it's Nova Scotia next.

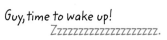

Guy, time to wake up!
Zzzzzzzzzzzzzzzzzzzzz.

GOOD MORNING, GUY!
Wha...? Oh, yeah....

We're going to Nova Scotia today, remember? You're coming.
Can't it wait until morning?

It IS morning.
Okay, okay. I'm getting up!

Good!
Zzzzzzzzzzzzzzzzzzzzz.

Things We'll Do and Places We'll Go Next Time

1. Okay, we'll drive our car up Magnetic Hill. We'll really do it this time. Honest!

2. Rappel off the 40 m (130 ft.) vertical cliffs at Cape Enrage. We won't look down.

3. We'll go to Chigneto Bay at the far end of the Bay of Fundy, where the tides will be the highest and the fastest.

4. Visit the seals and puffins on Machias Seal Island (and add more animals to my wildlife list).

5. Go to Hopewell Cape and play hide-and-seek among the "flowerpots" at low tide.

6. Try sea-kayaking at Saint Andrews, or go canoeing on the Miramichi or Saint John rivers.

7. We'll go to the Miramichi Folk Song Festival or the Highland Games and Scottish Festival in Fredericton and hear the music.

The Irish Festival at Miramichi

(It's a cover-up !)

Covered wooden bridges are a New Brunswick specialty. The bridges were covered so they would last longer.

Puffin

Smokin'! Smoked herring is a New Brunswick delicacy.

Seals at Machias Seal Island

At low tide, you can play hide-and-seek in the tunnels and caves around these rocks at Hopewell Cape. That's not such a hot idea at high tide, unless you are a fish.

Exceedingly Weird

At Magnetic Hill, in Moncton, cars seem to roll uphill all by themselves. It's very strange. The other strange thing is that neither Rachel nor I can remember going to Magnetic Hill, even though Mom says we did. She says we've been to so many places, sometimes it's hard to remember them all.

We really should take the kids to Magnetic Hill. It's a big tourist attraction.

Let's not and say we did. We'll buy a postcard of it.

Good idea.

99

Enough!

N•VA

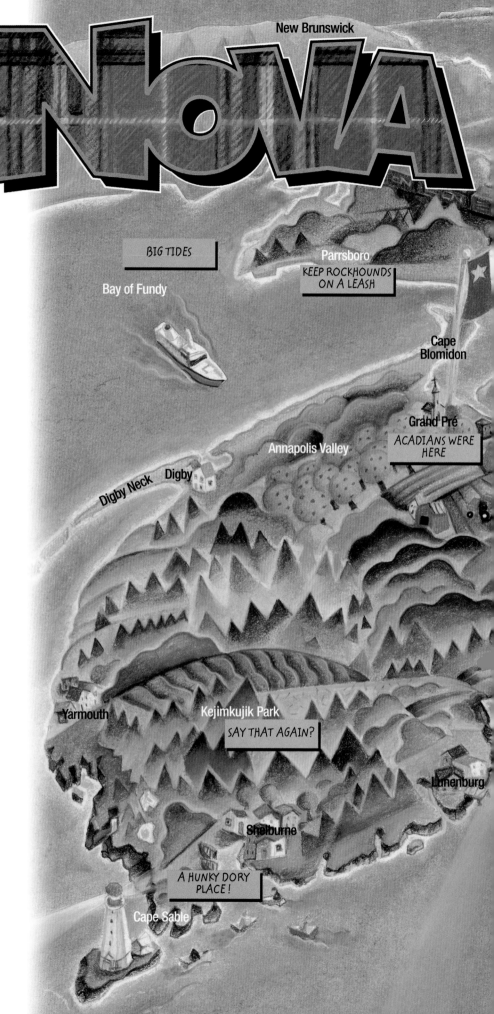

New Brunswick

BIG TIDES

Bay of Fundy

Parrsboro

KEEP ROCKHOUNDS
ON A LEASH

Cape
Blomidon

Grand Pré

ACADIANS WERE
HERE

Annapolis Valley

Digby Neck Digby

Yarmouth

Kejimkujik Park

SAY THAT AGAIN?

Lunenburg

Shelburne

A HUNKY DORY
PLACE!

Cape Sable

"Ciad Mile Failte!"

According to our tourist brochure, that means "one hundred thousand welcomes" in Gaelic. That's a lot of welcomes, but folks here are friendly.

Nova Scotia is almost an island—it's just hanging on to Canada by a narrow strip of land. Apparently, wherever you go in Nova Scotia, you are never more than 56 km (35 miles) from the sea.

Me—I plan to be *in* the sea as much as possible.

Provincial Flower
Mayflower

Provincial Arms

Provincial Flag

The Fundy Coast

Can I trade in my parents? When they're not making me learn about history, they're making me hike. And when they are not making me hike, they are making me eat scallops!

This morning we went to Grand Pré, where the French-speaking Acadians used to live before the British forced them to leave in 1755, burning their villages for good measure. When the Acadians fled their cherished homes around the Bay of Fundy, they were scattered far and wide, and friends and family never saw each other again, ever. Rachel got furious about it. I told her to simmer down, since it all happened a million years ago. Well, 250 years ago.

"It's still not right!" she yelled. Phew! Take cover when Rachel gets upset.

Then we visited Annapolis Royal, the longest-established town in the country. Its other claim to fame is that it's "the most fought-over place in Canada." (In our family, it's the front seat of the car.)

"What's here to fight about?" I asked.

"The British and French fought over who would have control of the New World," said Mom. "And who would make big bucks from cod fishing and the fur trade. This was one of the hot spots."

My teacher last year would have stepped in and said, "If you two can't work it out without fighting, *nobody* gets it!"

According to Mom

Life in Canada in the 1600s wasn't easy for British or French settlers. In 1605, at the French colony Port Royal, Samuel de Champlain started the Order of Good Cheer (actually, he called it L'Ordre de Bon Temps because he was French). Champlain, who came to be known as the "Father of New France," started the order to keep up the men's spirits and make sure they didn't get bored during the long, cold winter nights. They all took turns coming up with fun things to do in the evening, like feasting at banquets, performing plays, and singing songs.

This is a garage we saw painted like an Acadian flag. Despite the best attempts of the British to get rid of the Acadians in the 1700s, their numbers have continued to grow, and there are now nearly half a million Acadians in Atlantic Canada.

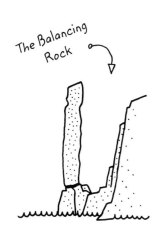

The Balancing Rock

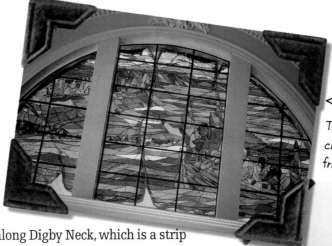

The stained glass windows in the church at Grand Pré show scenes from the deportation of the Acadians.

This afternoon, we drove along Digby Neck, which is a strip of land sticking way out into the ocean, and then we hiked a crazy trail with rope railings and stairs to the Balancing Rock. It's a gigantic, 7 m (23 ft.) high rock balanced precariously on the edge of a ledge, with waves crashing below. Don't count on it still being there when you visit; it's *really* close to falling. I was just itching to give it a shove.

We bought a bag of scallops from the dock at Digby for dinner. Scallops don't even taste that bad; they aren't going to kill you or anything. My mother, who ate most of mine, apparently agrees. We watched the ocean for whales, but they refused to perform.

Mom promises that tomorrow there will be absolutely no history, hiking, or scallops. (Think she can do it?) We're going to the beach—Mavillette Beach Provincial Park on the French Shore, where a lot of modern Acadians live.

Instructions to Make Your Own Postcard-perfect Fishing Village

1. START WITH A SHELTERED, ROCKY HARBOUR. ADD A DOCK—WEATHERED AND SAGGING.

2. MAKE A PLEASING ARRANGEMENT OF WOODEN HOUSES IN VARIOUS COLOURS AROUND THE HARBOUR.

3. PLUNK A FEW LITTLE WOODEN DORIES HERE AND THERE.

4. SPRAY YOUR VILLAGE WITH FISHY SMELL AND SEAGULL POOP.

5. ADD TOURISTS WITH CAMERAS. AT LEAST ONE PERSON WILL BE TALKING TO A VIDEO CAMERA.

6. THE PERFECT VILLAGE WILL HAVE A LIGHTHOUSE AT THE END OF THE POINT. OFFSHORE A HUMPBACK WHALE WILL BLOW.

7. OPTIONAL: INCLUDE A GIFT SHOP SELLING PLASTIC LOBSTERS AND LITTLE SHIPS STUCK IN BOTTLES.

Around Halifax

"Hunky Dory"

The Citadel

To: kheisler@relay.com
From: gbowers@galaxy.com
Subject: Pirates and stuff

Hi Kyle,
Too bad about your go-kart. Maybe you could build another one—with brakes this time?

I'm on the East Coast. We're visiting friends in Halifax. Remember we read about the Great Explosion of 1917, where a ship full of TNT blew up in Halifax Harbour? Almost 2,000 people were killed and half the city was demolished. It was the biggest explosion ever before the atom bomb was dropped on Japan in 1945. Well, it's a lot quieter here these days.

We spent the morning at the Maritime Museum, so I've seen lots of boats. The best was the World War II Corvette. We also saw the sailing ship that's on the Canadian dime—the *Bluenose*. Actually, what we saw was a replica—*Bluenose II*. Down at the harbour, we saw the warehouses where pirates used to store their loot. No kidding—real, ruthless, cut-throat pirates. Apparently, looting was a perfectly legitimate and very profitable business in those days.

At the top of Halifax is the Citadel, a fortress with walls all around. The British built it to keep the French out (I think there's a familiar theme here). I was sweating buckets by the time we'd climbed all the way up there! But I wasn't as hot as the guards wearing bearskin hats (called busbies) who were parading around. Are they nuts? Maybe the heat escaped through their knees, since they were wearing kilts.

At noon, we watched the soldiers shoot the cannon, and now I'm deaf. That's okay, given the number of bagpipes playing around town.

Yo,
Guy

At the Maritime Museum, we went on board the CSS Acadia and met Clara the cat. Her official title: Ship's Rodent Control Officer.

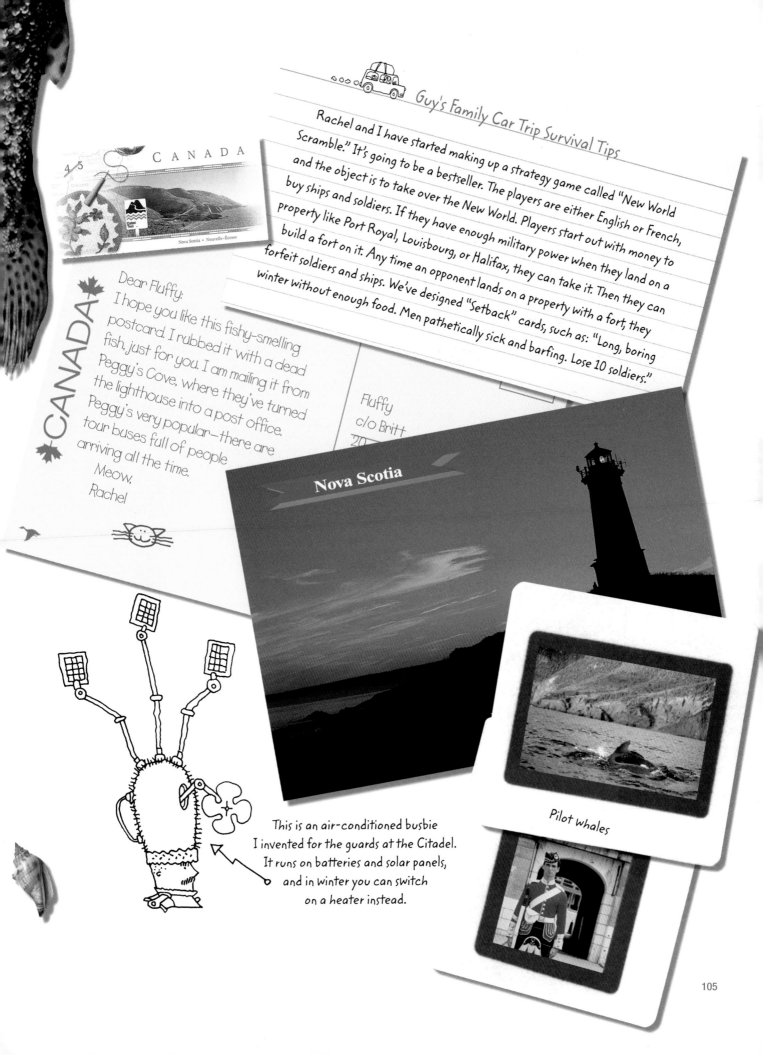

Rachel and I have started making up a strategy game called "New World Scramble." It's going to be a bestseller. The players are either English or French, and the object is to take over the New World. Players start out with money to buy ships and soldiers. If they have enough military power when they land on a property like Port Royal, Louisbourg, or Halifax, they can take it. Then they can build a fort on it. Any time an opponent lands on a property with a fort, they forfeit soldiers and ships. We've designed "Setback" cards, such as: "Long, boring winter without enough food. Men pathetically sick and barfing. Lose 10 soldiers."

C A N A D A

Nova Scotia · Nouvelle-Écosse

Dear Fluffy:
I hope you like this fishy-smelling postcard. I rubbed it with a dead fish, just for you. I am mailing it from Peggy's Cove, where they've turned the lighthouse into a post office. Peggy's very popular—there are tour buses full of people arriving all the time.
Meow,
Rachel

Fluffy
c/o Britt
20

Nova Scotia

This is an air-conditioned busbie I invented for the guards at the Citadel. It runs on batteries and solar panels, and in winter you can switch on a heater instead.

Pilot whales

Louisbourg, 1744

C'est moi, Guy LeBlanc. I'm a French soldier at Fortress Louisbourg, protecting the territory of New France against the British. I carry around a musket and a nasty-looking three-sided bayonet. I wear a wool coat and a three-sided hat with turned-up edges. (If it collects rainwater, I tilt my head and it pours out.) I keep watch for British invaders, eat cod stew, and never bathe. I get paid a pathetic wage.

As you may have guessed, we spent today at the Fortress of Louisbourg, on Cape Breton Island. It really existed, but what's here now is a reconstruction. The original fortress was a thriving seaport and the capital of Île Royal (Cape Breton Island). It was captured and burned about 250 years ago by the British—not once, but twice. But nobody knew that was going to happen in 1744, which is the date Louisbourg is stuck at today.

We almost didn't get in because Rachel was wearing a red T-shirt. Red is the English colour, and the guard accused her of being a spy. But she can talk her way out of anything. Once inside the walls, we wandered around town, chatting with soldiers and officers, blacksmiths, bakers, and other townspeople, all dressed in old-fashioned clothes and totally convinced it really is 1744.

Saddle-sore? If the soldiers did something wrong, their punishment was to have to sit on this horse for an hour a day with their hands tied behind their backs. The horse has a pointy back, so this was a very uncomfortable ride. o⎯⎯⎯⎯→

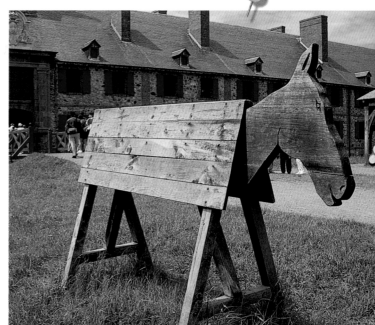

What's strange about these playing cards? Right! No numbers! The common people in Louisbourg were illiterate, so there was no point putting numbers on the cards; they couldn't read them.

Rachel decided she should have been an army drummer. The drummer knew all sorts of different beats that were used as commands to the soldiers in battle. He stood beside the general during the fighting so that when the general issued orders, the drummer would rat-tat-tat them to the troops. Rachel likes giving orders. Also, there was a kind of rule in battle that it was unsportsmanlike to shoot the drummer, so that was a good person to be.

The soldier who fired the cannon was not a good person to be. Not only was he an excellent enemy target, he could just as likely kill *himself* from accidental cannon explosions. (A common hazard when you're playing with gunpowder and hot cannonballs.)

The British didn't attack while we were there. That was disappointing, but the troops did fire a cannon for the tourists anyway. When we drove away, the Fortress of Louisbourg was still standing. I figure that if it survived Rachel, it should surely be able to survive a British attack.

Lifting a cannonball.

According to Mom

The first siege of Louisbourg was in 1745, when troops from New England (in the United States), helped by the British, attacked. They must have flunked Effective Battle Strategies 101. Listen to this:

The first night, the New Englanders were trying a night-time raid on the Island Battery (an island at the mouth of Louisbourg Harbour that the French had fortified with cannons and other guns), but their officers didn't show up. Another time, the moon was too bright, so they didn't have the cover of the darkness. They tried again, but this time the soldiers were too drunk. That's three strikes! When they finally successfully rowed out to the battery and landed in the dark, a not very bright soldier shouted out three cheers! This tipped off the French that they were being attacked, so they blasted the New Englanders, killing sixty men and taking 116 prisoner. Oops!

According to Dad

Here's something fishy. Want to know how to make a fortune in 1744? Diamonds? Beaver hats? Nope, try … cod! Salted and dried codfish was worth big money back in Europe. That was part of the reason for Fortress Louisbourg—France wanted to keep that cod fishery. Given the state of cod fishing today, the English might be wondering why they bothered attacking. Besides, have you ever tasted salted, dried cod?

Miners' Museum & Miners' Village Restaurant

VISIT AN UNDERGR COAL MIN

COAL IN NOVA SCOTIA
COAL
CAPE BRETON
Miners Museum

Coal from Glace Bay

↑
Addition to Rachel's rock collection

Down the Coal Mine

We're still on Cape Breton Island, and today I discovered what it would be like to be a coal miner. We went underground at a 1932 coal mine in Glace Bay. The mine tunnels go down, down, down under the ocean, following the seams of coal. Some go 16 km (10 miles) out, heading for Newfoundland. It's dark, damp, dirty, and dangerous down there. The tunnels are so low, adults have to stoop and even then they thunk the top of their hard hats.

Our tour guide was a retired miner who started working in a mine like this when he was 17 years old. His father and grandfather worked in the mine, too. They'd go down underground in the morning, shovel a tonne of coal into each cart, and get paid 68 cents a cart. They ate lunch down in the pit, too. Our guide said he used to tell his mother to pack him an extra sandwich to feed the rats. Yes, rats.

"You *want* there to be rats down there," he said. As long as the rats are there, that means the air in the mine is still okay to breathe. "If you see the rats leave, then you leave too, in a hurry."

Trouble was, the rats would eat his lunch. So he would throw his spare sandwich and watch the rats chase after it, then he'd gobble up the rest of his food before they came back.

According to Mom

You guessed it, Mom's also an expert on coal mining. This time I caught her reading and studying up on it before she wowed us with her knowledge. Here's what she told us:

1. Coal mining is still important in Nova Scotia, and there's lots more coal underground. In this province, they burn coal to generate electricity.

2. Even with modern mining techniques, disasters do still happen. At the Springhill Mine in 1958, there was a cave-in and 75 miners died. An explosion at the Westray Mine in 1992 killed 26 men. Eleven of the bodies were never recovered from underground.

3. Our tour guide told her that he had a small part in a movie called "Pit Pony," filmed in Glace Bay. (I read the book in school—maybe you did, too?)

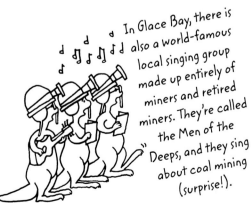

In Glace Bay, there is also a world-famous local singing group made up entirely of miners and retired miners. They're called the Men of the Deeps, and they sing about coal mining (surprise!).

There were ponies down in the mine too, to haul the carts of ore. During the 1930s mining, these pit ponies never came out of the pit and never saw the sun. Some life!

Our guide said you always had to watch out for a build-up of explosive gas in the mine. In the early days, they tested the air using canaries in cages. If the canary collapsed, it meant the gas was bad.

Once, our guide had a very near miss. At the last moment, he was given a different mining shift. There was an explosion that killed 12 miners on the shift he was supposed to have been on. He did lose brothers and uncles in other mining disasters. He said people kept on working in the mine because that was the only work they could find to feed their families.

The sun was shining when we came out of the mine. Boy, it felt good!

Guillemots are cool seabirds with red feet. To see them, we hiked all the way out to a point called Middle Point. From above, we watched them dive off the cliff ledges, swooping low over the water like mini jet-fighters, wings flapping at warp speed. Watch out, fish!

According to Dad

Everyone knows that Alexander Graham Bell invented the telephone, right? Well, Dad says that's only one of this famous Canadian's many incredible inventions. Are you wondering what else he invented?

How about kites that can carry people, one of the first gasoline-powered biplanes, a hydrofoil boat that set world speed records, a gizmo to get the salt out of seawater, ways to help teach deaf people, a breed of superior sheep, a phonograph, an iron lung for underwater divers, medical devices, electrical devices, and lots of other useful and useless stuff. You can see lots of these inventions at the Alexander Graham Bell Museum in Baddeck, a town on the Bras d'Or Lake where Bell spent many summers.

Guy's Wildlife List
Guillemots

Exceedingly Weird

I found an alien-monster snail, called a nudibranch. It doesn't have a shell, and part of its guts stick out and wave around. Apparently, nudibranches eat things that can sting, like jellyfish, then absorb the stinging cells into their guts. So anything that touches those protruding bits of gut gets zapped! Bizarre.

We found these insect-gobbling pitcher plants in a bog. Since bogs aren't very nutritious, some plants eat insects to get extra goodies. Pitcher plants are shaped like jugs, open at the top. Insects slide down hairs on the inside of the leaves to the bottom, where there's no escape! If the insects are lucky, it's death by drowning in collected rainwater. Otherwise, they are slowly digested by the plant's enzymes. Remember this for your next horror movie.

"Farewell to Nova Scotia, the sea-bound coast..."

Rachel's learned a new song to add to her repertoire. It must be my lucky day! She's practicing "Farewell to Nova Scotia" for when we take the ferry to Newfoundland. (It's a 13-hour ferry ride, which allows lots of time for singing.) Now, if only I could learn the bagpipes in my last few hours here, maybe I could drown her out. . . .

Things We'll Do and Places We'll Go Next Time

1. We'll go canoeing in Kejimkujik National Park.

2. Hike to the end of Cape Blomidon. Make sure the wind doesn't blow-me-down.

3. Rachel wants to go to Partridge Island near Parrsboro to find amethysts and agates on the beach at low tide. The Bay of Fundy tides do all the digging, so you just have to go down at low tide to see what's been uncovered.

4. Watch the tide come in at the entrance to Cobequid Bay, at the head of the Bay of Fundy, where there are the highest recorded tides in the world (16.5 m / 54 ft.).

5. Mom wants to go to a ceilidh (pronounced kay-lee). It's a musical concert where people play guitars, fiddles, accordions, bagpipes—whatever. That shouldn't be hard to find; there's music everywhere in Nova Scotia.

6. Dad wants to watch the Highland Summer Games in Antigonish. (Warning: May contain excessive bagpipe music.) He says he wants to see a caber toss. That's a long, heavy pole tossed as a test of strength.

7. I don't want to go anywhere they make me eat haggis again.

This sign was at the docks in Pleasant Bay, Cape Breton Island.

PLEASANT. BAY
FiSH. LTD.
PHONE

Food I Was Introduced to for My Own Good

Today I tasted haggis. I lived to tell the tale. Imagine a combination of sheep's liver, heart, and lungs, chopped up and boiled with fat and oatmeal. It's a Scottish specialty that people here try on unsuspecting tourists. It tastes . . . um, indescribable.

A cool gift shop inside a giant lobster trap in Cheticamp, Cape Breton Island

A: Whut is a "gut"?

   B: It's a narrow waterway, like an inlet.

A: You've gut to be kidding!

   B: I'm not! Nova Scotia has luts of guts. There's a South Gut at St. Ann's, for example.

A: Gut Grief, what next!

The Cape Breton Highlands look a lot like the Highlands of Scotland. Apparently this makes Scottish highlanders homesick.

According to Mom

Mom told us about Glooscap, the legendary hero of the Mi'kmaq people. According to tradition, Glooscap lived at Cape Blomidon, at the top end of the Bay of Fundy. Huge and powerful, he is said to have created natural land features in this area. He must have had quite the temper! When he was angry, he chucked enormous clumps of earth into the bay and made new islands. That's how the Five Islands (Moose, Diamond, Long, Egg, and Pinnacle) were formed.

Bucko Beaver has had about enough of travelling!

AT 12 NOON, OUR FAVOURITE RODENT BLASTS OFF FROM THE ATLANTIC. HIS MISSION: TO REACH THE PACIFIC BEFORE NOON. (IN OTHER WORDS, TO GET THERE BEFORE LEAVING HERE.)

OH NO! JUST OUTSIDE OF MOOSE JAW, OUR HERO IS SWEPT UP BY A PRAIRIE TORNADO, SUCKED INTO THE SWIRLING VORTEX. THE TORNADO SPITS HIM OUT IN FORT MCMURRAY! OFF COURSE, BIG TIME!

THINKING QUICKLY, BUCKO BEAVER DONS SPECIAL BREATHING APPARATUS AND TAKES THE SHORTEST ROUTE BACK —WHOOSH—THROUGH THE OIL PIPELINES SOUTH TO REGINA.

DRIPPING OIL, BB THUNDERS TO THE PACIFIC FINISH LINE, ARRIVING IN VANCOUVER THREE HOURS AND FIFTY-SEVEN MINUTES AFTER HE STARTED (AND EXACTLY THREE MINUTES BEFORE NOON). SUCCESS!

FINISH

(Let's hear it for time zones.)

Ungava Bay

Quebec

Happy Vall
Goose Ba

I am lurching back and forth on this great big overnight ferry to Newfoundland. We just went out on deck, and through the dark and foggy night we saw huge waves. Scary stuff! The foghorn sounds so often, I've perfected a pretty good imitation. "Bleeeeeeeeee-yermph." We have laid out our sleeping bags on the floor of our cabin, and Mom is trying to persuade Rachel that the swaying is just like rocking a baby to sleep in a cradle. Lurch, crash! Lurch, crash! Nice try, Mom.

They say that somewhere out here in the fog is "the Rock," also known as Newfoundland. I guess we'll know when we hit it.

 Provincial Arms

 Provincial Flower
Pitcher Plant

 Provincial Flag

A WHALE OF A
TIME HERE

UNDLAND & LABRADOR

LABRADOR

Atlantic Ocean

Red Bay

L'Anse aux Meadows

Strait of Belle Isle

A COOL PLACE

Twillingate

THE MATTHEW

Port aux Choix

Gros Morne National Park

BEOTHUKS WERE ONCE HERE

YE OLDE ROCKS

NEWFOUNDLAND

St. John's

Corner Brook

Cape Spear

COUNTRY ENDS TURN AROUND

of St. Lawence

Channel Port-aux-Basques

Cape St. Mary's

SEABIRD RAVE

HIBERNIA OIL FIELD

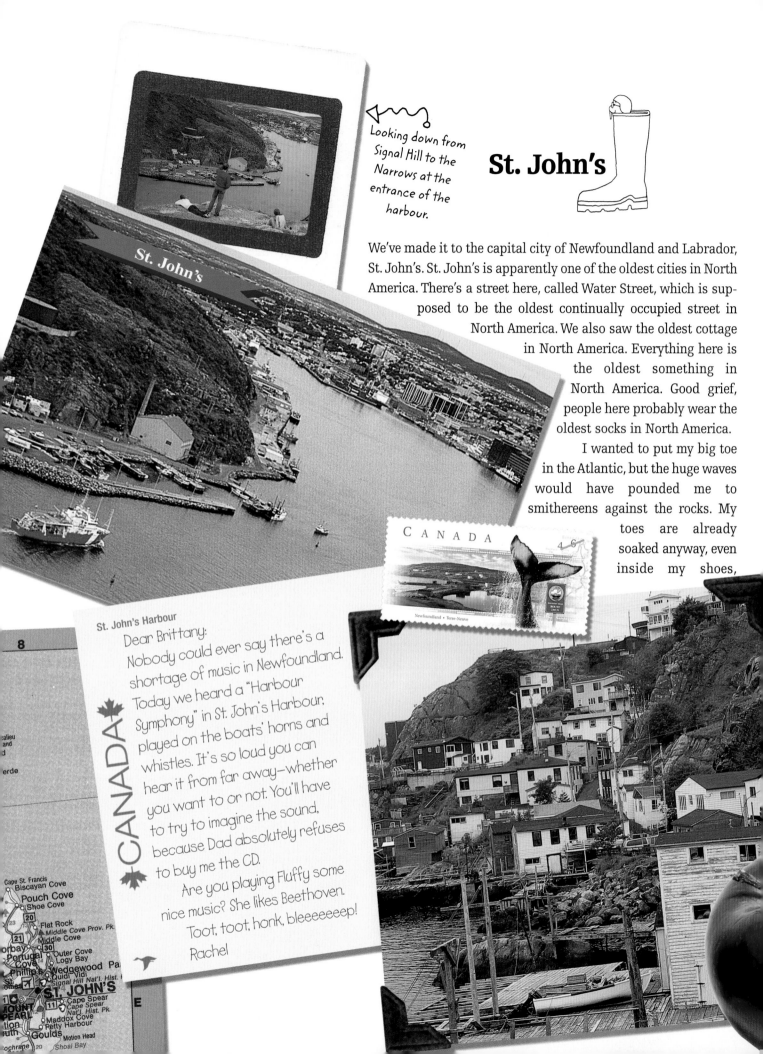

Looking down from Signal Hill to the Narrows at the entrance of the harbour.

St. John's

We've made it to the capital city of Newfoundland and Labrador, St. John's. St. John's is apparently one of the oldest cities in North America. There's a street here, called Water Street, which is supposed to be the oldest continually occupied street in North America. We also saw the oldest cottage in North America. Everything here is the oldest something in North America. Good grief, people here probably wear the oldest socks in North America.

I wanted to put my big toe in the Atlantic, but the huge waves would have pounded me to smithereens against the rocks. My toes are already soaked anyway, even inside my shoes,

St. John's Harbour

Dear Brittany:
Nobody could ever say there's a shortage of music in Newfoundland. Today we heard a "Harbour Symphony" in St. John's Harbour, played on the boats' horns and whistles. It's so loud you can hear it from far away—whether you want to or not. You'll have to try to imagine the sound, because Dad absolutely refuses to buy me the CD.
Are you playing Fluffy some nice music? She likes Beethoven.
Toot, toot, honk, bleeeeeeep!
Rachel

CANADA

CANADA 46

Newfoundland • Terre-Neuve

Here's the path we walked from Signal Hill down to St. John's.

because of the rain. We're constantly getting soaked here. Mom should have packed gumboots.

Don't get me wrong, St. John's is great! The narrow, hilly streets around the harbour are crowded with wooden houses, all painted different colours, clinging to the rock. Everything looks like it's taken a beating from the weather. Winter storms here must be quite something.

We went up Signal Hill—a very big hunk of rock. It's high above the channel that ships go through to get into St. John's Harbour. Its position makes it a perfect spot for dropping cannon balls on enemy warships coming through the Narrows (the passage into the harbour). Going back to the 1800s, the British did it to the French, then the French did it to the British, then the British . . . then the French . . . then British . . . You get the picture. All I kept thinking was, it would be one wild go-kart ride down this hill!

We also took a ferry to Bell Island, which once had the largest iron ore mine in the world. It received a direct hit during the Second World War from German submarines. Today, you can climb on the remains of one of the wrecked ships beached in the shallow water. You can slip and get your only dry shoes soaked, and get a lecture from your mother.

Cape Spear

This is the most easterly point in North America— Cape Spear. For a few moments we were the most easterly human beings on the continent of North America.

Exceedingly Weird

And I thought the rest of Canada had strange place names! We all chose our favourite Newfoundland ones today.

My favourite: Badger or Witless Bay (I can't decide)

Rachel's favourite: Twillingate

Mom's favourite: Heart's Content or Come By Chance

Dad's favourite: Main Tickle

Kayaking and other Newfoundlandish Stuff

Yesterday, we went sea kayaking and saw lots of puffins. Puffins are cool! No wonder Newfoundland decided they would make a good provincial bird. However, puffins can't fly for beans. That's tough when you're a bird. It's the take-off that they have trouble with. They can launch off cliffs, but to take off from the water, they need a good head wind. We watched their frantic flapping as they tried to get airborne and gain altitude. We yelled positive encouragement: "I think you can. I think you can! YOU DID IT!"

According to our kayaking guide, puffins actually use their wings and "fly" much better under water.

We rode the wave swells through tunnels in the rock and into deep caves, and landed for lunch on a sheltered beach with a huge waterfall. As we scrambled on the rocks we saw these large, shadowy blobs moving in the water. They were schools of little fish called capelin, a whale's favourite fast food. Where there are capelin, there are probably whales. Sure enough, in the distance, we saw several humpback whales surfacing and blowing. What with the capelin attracting the whales, and the whales attracting tourists in cruise boats and kayaks, it was quite busy out there on the water.

Coming back against the wind and waves was a grunt! The puffins weren't the only ones who were puffin'. I was in the front of a kayak with Mom, getting soaked by waves landing in my lap, while wind gusts almost blew us backwards across the Atlantic. It's for times like this that they invented motors.

"It's a dog-gone, cod-darned shame..."

According to Dad

Newfoundland is very fishy. If you don't like the smell of fish, stay in Saskatchewan. People work, eat, sing, and talk of fish. Especially codfish. They have been fishing for cod for generations. Trouble is, the cod have been overfished. And now the government has banned cod fishing. People still fish for shrimp, lobster, and crab, but it isn't the same. Now people sing about how sad it is that there's no cod. It goes to show, maybe you can stop Newfoundlanders from cod fishing, but you can't stop them from singing.

Capelin eggs on the beach where we had lunch

Puffin' puffin

Exceedingly Weird

Avast, ye hearties! Here be pirates! No kidding—there was a real pirate, Peter Easton (is that any name for a pirate?), who lived in Harbour Grace around 1610. He was the terror of the coast, raiding ships and plundering villages, just like pirates are supposed to. Eventually he became filthy rich, carted all his loot back to Europe, and lived in a castle.

According to Mom

Everyone knows that Christopher Columbus sailed the ocean blue in fourteen hundred ninety-two. But it's another explorer, John Cabot, who Newfoundlanders really kick up their heels for. Newfoundlanders celebrate Cabot's 1497 landing at Bonavista, Newfoundland. Funny thing: Nova Scotians celebrate the same thing in northern Cape Breton Island. Other people say the landing actually happened in St. John's. Or farther south in the United States. Since nobody knows for sure, you can buy souvenirs of Cabot's ship, *The Matthew*, everywhere. That John Cabot —he knew how to set up a good tourist scam.

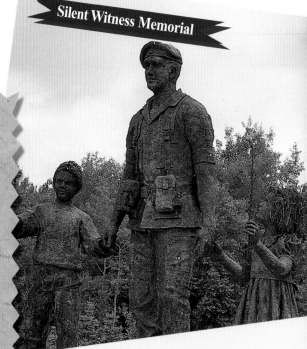

Silent Witness Memorial

CANADA

Dear Brittany:
This statue is at the site of Canada's worst airplane crash. You can still see where the crashing plane wiped out an enormous area of forest. It went down just after taking off from Gander's airport in December 1985. The passengers, 248 United States soldiers going home for Christmas, were killed along with the eight crew members. Now the site is called the Silent Witness Memorial.
   So sad! Give Fluffy a hug for me.
   Your friend, Rachel

This is a replica of *The Matthew*, John Cabot's ship. It looks pretty small for a transatlantic crossing— no on-board shuffleboard, for example.

Didn't the Vikings land in Newfoundland 500 years before Cabot?

Actually, Native people were here in Newfoundland thousands of years before the Vikings.

So, does this whole "I got here first" business seem a little pointless?

It's just a "human" thing. They have to mark their territory.

117

Gros Morne

We're across on the other side of the island of Newfoundland now, camped in Gros Morne National Park, right above the beach. After driving through forests, forests, and yet more forests (it was a long drive), we have arrived on what looks like Arctic barrens. No trees except some poor stunted, wind-blasted ones with a permanent lean, called tuckamore. Actually, if this wind doesn't stop sometime I'm going to be tuckamored myself.

"This park has really interesting geology," said Mom, the guidebook reader.

"But does it have flush toilets?" Rachel wanted to know.

The guidebook explanation was complicated, but Dad provided us with his kid-friendly geology lesson. "It's like this: A long, long time ago, two huge continental plates smacked into each other, making a mess of the landscape like you wouldn't believe. Everything upside down, sideways, and inside out."

"Sounds like how the kitchen looks when Guy cooks," said Rachel.

"Worse," said Dad. "Land that was once at the bottom of the sea ended up on top of cliffs. Old stuff from deep inside the earth got shoved out to the top."

"So now geologists can study billion-year-old rock from deep inside the earth, which they otherwise couldn't get to," said Mom.

"Fascinating," said Rachel. "What about the flush toilets?"

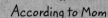

According to Mom

Mom told us about Beothuks today. They were the Native people who had been living here in Newfoundland before the Europeans arrived. But they were all wiped out! The Europeans brought guns, diseases, and an attitude that spelled bad news for the Beothuks. Sometimes the Beothuks were shot like unwanted animals. When there were almost none left, scientists started capturing and studying them. As if they were an interesting, endangered species! The last Beothuk, a girl named Shanawdithit, died in captivity in 1829. In captivity!

Bakeapple berries

Partridgeberries

Food I Was Introduced to for My Own Good

It poured with rain tonight so we went to a restaurant for dessert. Dad had bakeapple cheesecake. Bakeapples are little golden berries that look like yellow raspberries but taste more like sour peaches. We saw lots in the bog. Mom had partridgeberry pie, which is another bog plant that looks like a cranberry. Rachel and I had chocolate milkshakes that did not come from a bog (we hope).

The profile of the
Old Man of the Mountain

Can you see him?

This afternoon we took a boat trip on Western Brook Pond in the park. I should explain that Newfoundlanders call all lakes "ponds," no matter how huge. This one was shaped like a deep trench with 700 m (2,295 ft.) cliffs going straight up and waterfalls pouring down. The tour guide explained about the land here springing up after being squished down during the last ice age, and glaciers cutting down through the raised land to make this deep trench. Well, something like that. The guide also pointed out faces you could see in the rocks—like the profile of the Old Man of the Mountain.

To get to the boat dock, we had to hike 3 km (2 miles) on boardwalks across a bog. The bog was full of carnivorous, insect-devouring plants, like sundews and pitcher plants (Newfoundland's official plant). We also saw a moose! I like moose because they look so ridiculous.

Guy's Wildlife List
Newfoundland moose

Exceedingly Weird

This is what I found out about the weird and wonderful moose.

1. Moose are nosy. Most of the inside of that long face with the droopy end is nose.

2. A moose can weigh more than four refrigerators.

3. A moose has four stomachs.

4. A moose has long, skinny legs. Newborn calves have a hard time getting them under control.

5. A moose has valves in its nostrils. They keep out water when the moose dives under water looking for pond weed. (Hey, you need to eat something if you have four stomachs!)

6. A moose's two eyes work independently. He only needs one to see you.

How to Make a Squishy Bog

1. START WITH SOIL FULL OF PEAT— THAT SOFT, SPONGY SOIL THAT YOU PUT IN PLANT POTS BECAUSE IT HOLDS WATER WELL. THAT WILL MAKE YOUR BOG NICE AND MUSHY.

2. ADD INTERESTING PLANTS: CARNIVOROUS PLANTS ARE HIGHLY RECOMMENDED. SINCE THERE ARE SO FEW NUTRIENTS IN YOUR BOG SOIL, THESE PLANTS WILL EAT INSECTS INSTEAD (CANADA FOOD GUIDE APPROVED).

3. AS THE PLANTS DIE, THEY WON'T DECAY. THERE'S TOO MUCH ACID AND NOT ENOUGH OXYGEN IN YOUR BOG. INSTEAD, DEAD PLANTS JUST PILE UP AND ADD TO THE STUFF IN THE BOG, SO IT GETS THICKER.

4. THE WATER FROM YOUR BOG SHOULD BE BROWN, FULL OF STUFF CALLED TANNIN. NEWFOUNDLAND HAS LOTS OF BROWN CREEKS AND WATERFALLS FLOWING DOWN FROM BOGS. (THEY DON'T TELL YOU THAT IN THE TOURIST BROCHURES!)

5. WATCH AS THE RISING BOG STARTS TO CREEP INTO NEARBY FORESTS, DROWNING THE ROOTS AND KILLING THE TREES. IS THIS SCARY OR WHAT?

6. BUILD A BOARDWALK ACROSS YOUR BOG AND PUT UP INTERPRETIVE SIGNS. TOURISTS LOVE THE IDEA OF INSECT-EATING PLANTS.

7. OH—ONE MORE THING: LET LOOSE A MOOSE IN YOUR BOG. ASK HIM TO PLEASE NOT WALK ALONG THE BOARDWALK, BECAUSE HE EXCEEDS THE WEIGHT ALLOWANCE.

A Norse farmer shared some Norse facts with me.

1. The Norsemen bathed in the freezing-cold creek once a week. They were cleaner than other Europeans of the time, who wore their underwear until it rotted off. (Where were their mothers!)

2. Norsemen figured groundwater made them sick, which it often did because they dumped their sewage water right beside their drinking water. Instead of drinking water, Norsemen drank beer and ale. Even the children drank weak beer.

3. Norsemen propped themselves up to sleep. That's because from the time they were born they lived in smoky houses and got lung diseases. They couldn't breathe very well when they were lying flat.

4. Norsemen called the Native people Skraelings, which means "wretched," which wasn't a compliment. There's no record of what rude names the Natives called the Norsemen.

Vikings, Labrador, and Icebergs

When we woke up yesterday morning, Mom said, "Shall I tell you what's in store for today?"

"Just as long as we don't have to learn anything," I said. Then I gave her a grin, just to show I was kidding. (Sort of.)

"We're going to see the spot where real, live Vikings landed in North America," she said.

"Not fake, dead Vikings?" asked Rachel. Poor Mom. Sometimes we are horrible children.

Off we went to L'Anse aux Meadows, at the northern tip of Newfoundland. We visited a reconstructed Viking house that was covered in thick slabs of sod cut out of the peat bogs. A sod house is just like covering your house with a lawn (but without any pink flamingo lawn ornaments). The Norseman I met inside said that the men who built these houses weren't actually "Vikings" at all. Vikings were the young Norse hoodlums who went off to plunder, pillage, and generally cause trouble. The Norsemen who landed here were seafarers and farmers, and much better behaved.

In the evening we drove to Fishing Point, near the town of St. Anthony's. There's a reconstructed sod house there, too. We could have eaten a great Viking feast, served by reconstructed Vikings, but I don't think they serve macaroni and cheese at great Viking feasts. So we went to the café instead, where it was on the menu. (My mother just shook her head in disbelief. Some days she can't figure out where I came from.)

A friendly Norseman and Dad

I've spent all day in a fog. Apparently, we were in Labrador today, but I haven't got the foggiest notion what it looks like. We took the ferry from Newfoundland across the Strait of Belle Isle to Labrador in the fog. We saw Atlantic Canada's largest lighthouse looming in the fog.

At the end of the road we found Red Bay. About 450 years ago it was the whaling capital of the world. The whalers came from the Basque coast, a region in France and Spain. These Basque whalers, in puny little boats, went out to sea looking for enormous whales. You can guess who won. The whale hunt was dangerous for the whalers, but it was definitely more dangerous for the whales. About 10,000 of them ended up as whale oil for lamps in Europe.

This evening, when we were back on the island of Newfoundland, the fog lifted and we saw icebergs just offshore! Huge, bluish white masses, almost ghostly, drifting or slowly turning in the current. Some of them were as big as a two-storey house. Occasionally a chunk would fall off, and it sounded like an explosion.

"You don't want to go too close," warned a fisherman we met on the dock. "Imagine coming across one of those in the fog. Even though they look big, they're eight times bigger under water. Sometimes they flip right over and make huge waves."

Restaurants here sell drinks with iceberg ice cubes in them. Imagine, 12,000-year-old ice in your pop. Some liquor companies tow Newfoundland icebergs to shore and use the "pure" water for making vodka. Rachel and I decided we should form the Iceberg Liberation Society and free all captured icebergs. They should be allowed to float and melt in peace without being hunted or harassed. Enough of this greed and profit.

Free the icebergs!

"Red alert! Family incoming. Take up attack positions."

Farewell, Atlantic Canada!

We've travelled from the Pacific to the Atlantic coast. We've sampled mosquitoes in all of Canada's ten provinces. Are we done?

Are you kidding? Not while there's more of Canada to be discovered. It's time to head for Canada's northern territories. Arctic Ocean—here we come!

"There won't be any mosquitoes up there, right?"

"Well. . ."

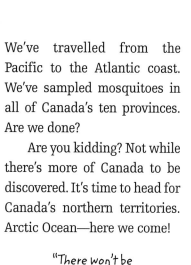

Things We'll Do and Places We'll Go Next Time

1. See the New Founde Lande Trinity Pageant in Trinity.

2. Discover where John Cabot landed (or might have landed) at Cape Bonavista.

3. Take a boat out to iceberg alley, near Twillingate, and see more icebergs.

4. Take in some of the many folk music festivals around the Rock.

5. Visit the gannets at St. Mary's Sea Bird Sanctuary. Take a boat out to Witless Bay to see, hear, and smell over two million seabirds. Phew!

6. Ride ferries to Newfoundland's outport villages, which you can't get to by road.

7. Take the ferry to Happy Valley/Goose Bay and explore more of Labrador. Not in the fog, this time.

8. Eat cod tongue. I promise I'll do that next time.

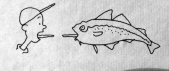

122

Bergy bits and growlers are the smaller bits of glaciers. Small is a relative word—bergy bits are the size of a car. The name "growler" comes from the sound the ice makes when it breaks off and falls to the sea.

Newfoundland crab

Sea slug

CAPTURED! AN ICEBERG IS TOWED AWAY, DESPITE THE ANGUISHED CRIES OF THE GROWLERS AND BERGY BITS LEFT BEHIND.

ICEBERG TOW CO.

DESPAIR NOT! UNDER COVER OF FOG, OUR FEARLESS HERO GLIDES SILENTLY TOWARD THE ICEBERG. HIS MISSION: TO GNAW THROUGH THE ROPES AND LIBERATE THE CAPTIVE BERG.

FREE THE BERGS!

BUT WAIT! A DARK SHADOW MOVES ACROSS THE WATER. IS IT . . . THE DARK SIDE OF THE OCEAN? THE BLOB FROM THE DEEP? WATCH OUT, BUCKO!

IT'S A SCHOOL OF CAPELIN! FOLLOWED BY A HUNGRY HUMPBACK! TOTAL CHAOS! NEVER A DULL DAY IN NEWFOUNDLAND!

NO PUFFIN' PLEASE! NEWFOUNDLAND

CAMPFIRE CHAT

Sneezing in Other Languages

"Ah . . . ah . . . ah . . . choooooo!"

Rachel sneezes like nobody else! She almost blew out the campfire.

"Still got your socks on?" asked Dad.

"Gesundheit!" said Mom.

"Why do you always say that?" Rachel asked.

"Gesundheit? It's German for 'good health,'" said Mom. "It's the expression your opa always used."

"Opa was German?"

"Yes, your grandfather came to Canada from Germany. You have lots of relatives there. Some day we'll go to visit them."

"Assuming we ever finish this trip," I said.

"So I'm part German?" Rachel asked.

"The part that sneezes," said Dad.

"You're also part Scottish, part English, and a bit of Ukrainian, too, if you go back far enough," said Mom.

"And part cocker spaniel."

"Daddy!"

"On your mother's side."

"You're just a typical Canadian, I guess," continued Mom. "A cultural mixed bag, with ancestors who immigrated to Canada sometime in the past."

"People still immigrate to Canada," I said. "Remember Moe, the new person in our class at school? He came from India."

"Oh, poor guy. Didn't anyone warn him about your teacher?" Rachel asked.

"Canada is known as a multicultural society, or a cultural mosaic," said Mom. "That means that lots of different cultures fit together to make the whole picture of Canadian society. Canadians are lucky because they can learn about other cultures without having to travel all around the world."

"Not to mention all the different ethnic foods we get to eat," said Dad.

"It probably helps to have a multicultural stomach," I said.

"Remember Chinatown in Vancouver and Toronto?" said Rachel. "And the poutine in Quebec? I ah . . . ah . . . ah . . . ah. . ."

"Look out, everyone!"

"Ah . . . ah . . . ah. . ."

"Take cover!"

"AH-CHOOOO!"

"Gesundheit!" said Mom.

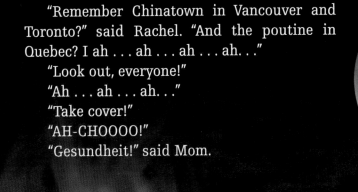

We're up north! Well, actually, we're down north. Dad says north is not really up, even though the Northwest Territories looks quite "up" to me on a map of Canada. You can tell north is "down" because the rivers flowing north through the territories are headed downhill to the Arctic Ocean.

Dad says this will all make more sense if I stand on my head.

(Psssst! Watch out for polar bears. They are all over the roads up here!)

EXPLORE CANADA'S ARCTIC
32875
NORTHWEST TERRITORIES
97
OCT

Territorial Arms

Territorial Flag

Territorial Flower
Mountain Avens

Arctic Ocean

Beaufort Sea

OIL HERE

Mackenzie Delta

PINGOS!

Inuvik

Aklavik

Yukon

Norman Wells

OIL HERE

Mackenzie River

South Nahanni River

MEGA WATERFALL

Virginia Falls

Canoeing on Hidden Lake

BUCKO BEAVER IS PADDLING THROUGH THE NORTHWEST TERRITORIES. AS THE TAIGA FORESTS GIVE WAY TO THE BARRENLANDS, HE REVELS IN THE SERENITY AND ISOLATION OF THE WILDERNESS, FAR, FAR FROM THE CROWDS.

According to Dad

There are diamonds in N. W. T.! The first diamond mine in N. W. T. opened in 1998 at Lac de Gras, about 300 km (185 miles) north of Yellowknife. Since then, other companies have started digging up diamonds in the North. When diamonds come out of the ground they are "diamonds in the rough". They look like worn-down glass that's been in the ocean for a long time. They aren't sparkling and glittering until they've been cut and polished.

We've been on a canoe trip on Hidden Lake, about 30 km (19 miles) from Yellowknife. It was hidden, but we found it. We've camped here for three days, all by ourselves. Except for Dad's snoring, it is very peaceful. When Rachel tipped the canoe, we discovered the water was quite warm. The weather has been downright hot, not what I expected in the Northwest Territories.

The drive north toward Yellowknife was long. We crossed the mighty Mackenzie River on a ferry. The river is huge and fast-flowing, and it still has about 1,800 km (1,120 miles) to go before it reaches the Arctic Ocean. In total, it's 4,241 km (2,635 miles), which makes it the longest river in Canada.

The local Dene call the river Deh Cho, which means "Big River." In 1789, the explorer Alexander Mackenzie called it the River of Disappointment. The poor guy paddled the river looking for a route to the Pacific Ocean but he ended up at the Arctic Ocean. So, really, why was the river renamed after Mackenzie?

WATCH OUT! HORDES OF MIGRATING CARIBOU BLOCK THE RIVER DOWNSTREAM! BB IS STUCK HERE FOR DAYS AND IS GETTING HUNGRIER. THERE ARE NO TREES TO MUNCH ON IN THE BARRENS. CRACK! BB CRACKS HIS TEETH ON A ROCK THAT'S HARDER THAN A ROCK. IT'S ... A DIAMOND. BUCKO HAS DISCOVERED A NEW DIAMOND DEPOSIT IN THE N.W.T.

We darned near got run over by bison early this morning. Suddenly Mom braked as these huge, dark shapes loomed out of the fog. They were quite strange-looking and most impressive. They are very big beasts with large, shaggy heads hanging down and a big hump between the shoulders.

"I've got to get a picture of this," said Dad, grabbing his camera and starting to get out of the car.

"I've read that bison can gallop at up to 60 km (37 miles) an hour when they are agitated," said Mom. "Apparently they are easily agitated."

Dad paused, then rolled down his window instead and took some photos. We waited politely until all the bison finished plodding across the road. Obviously, we had reached the bison sanctuary we'd read about.

Ferry crossing the Deh Cho

The Mackenzie Delta

Bison calf

Guy's Wildlife List
Wood bison

After we found our way out of Hidden Lake, we went to Cameron Falls and saw this sign. Yikes!

(No caribou yet! Dad says I'm in the wrong place at the wrong time.)

129

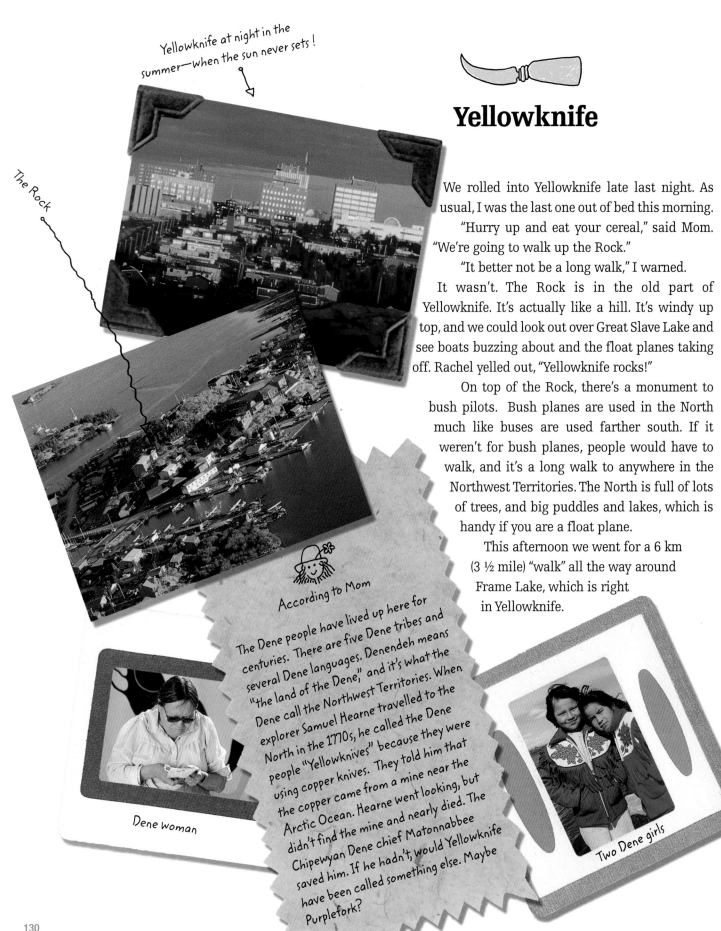

Yellowknife at night in the summer—when the sun never sets !

The Rock

Yellowknife

We rolled into Yellowknife late last night. As usual, I was the last one out of bed this morning.

"Hurry up and eat your cereal," said Mom. "We're going to walk up the Rock."

"It better not be a long walk," I warned.

It wasn't. The Rock is in the old part of Yellowknife. It's actually like a hill. It's windy up top, and we could look out over Great Slave Lake and see boats buzzing about and the float planes taking off. Rachel yelled out, "Yellowknife rocks!"

On top of the Rock, there's a monument to bush pilots. Bush planes are used in the North much like buses are used farther south. If it weren't for bush planes, people would have to walk, and it's a long walk to anywhere in the Northwest Territories. The North is full of lots of trees, and big puddles and lakes, which is handy if you are a float plane.

This afternoon we went for a 6 km (3 ½ mile) "walk" all the way around Frame Lake, which is right in Yellowknife.

According to Mom

The Dene people have lived up here for centuries. There are five Dene tribes and several Dene languages. Denendeh means "the land of the Dene," and it's what the Dene call the Northwest Territories. When explorer Samuel Hearne travelled to the North in the 1770s, he called the Dene people "Yellowknives" because they were using copper knives. They told him that the copper came from a mine near the Arctic Ocean. Hearne went looking, but didn't find the mine and nearly died. The Chipewyan Dene chief Matonnabbee saved him. If he hadn't, would Yellowknife have been called something else. Maybe Purplefork?

Dene woman

Two Dene girls

We saw loons and muskrat in the lake. But it was exhausting. The only thing that kept me going was that the mosquitoes attacked me every time I stopped.

Now we're going to dinner at the Wildcat Cafe. Dad's planning on ordering caribou meat. I'm campaigning for fries. Mom says we have to have a shower first. That's an outrage! Kids shouldn't have to get clean when they are camping!

WILD CAT CAFE

Yellowknife, N.W.T.

CANADA

Dear Brittany:
Here's a real polar bear we saw. Unfortunately, it's not a real live polar bear. But at least it didn't attack us. It was at the Prince of Wales Northern Heritage Centre.
We could touch all kinds of differ-ent animal fur there—like muskrat, muskox, arctic wolf, and arctic hare. Speaking of fur, how's my furry feline friend faring?
Your far-off, far-out, far-North, far-fetched friend, R a c h e l

Britt
20 R
Vict
V3

Polar Bear Exhibit at the Prince of Wales Northern Heritage Centre, Yellowknife, Northwest Terrritories

Food I Was Introduced to for My Own Good

We went to a Dogrib Dene community for a traditional Dene lunch. We listened to drumming on a caribou-skin drum, then we cooked bannock (a kind of bread dough) on a stick over the fire. Excellent!

131

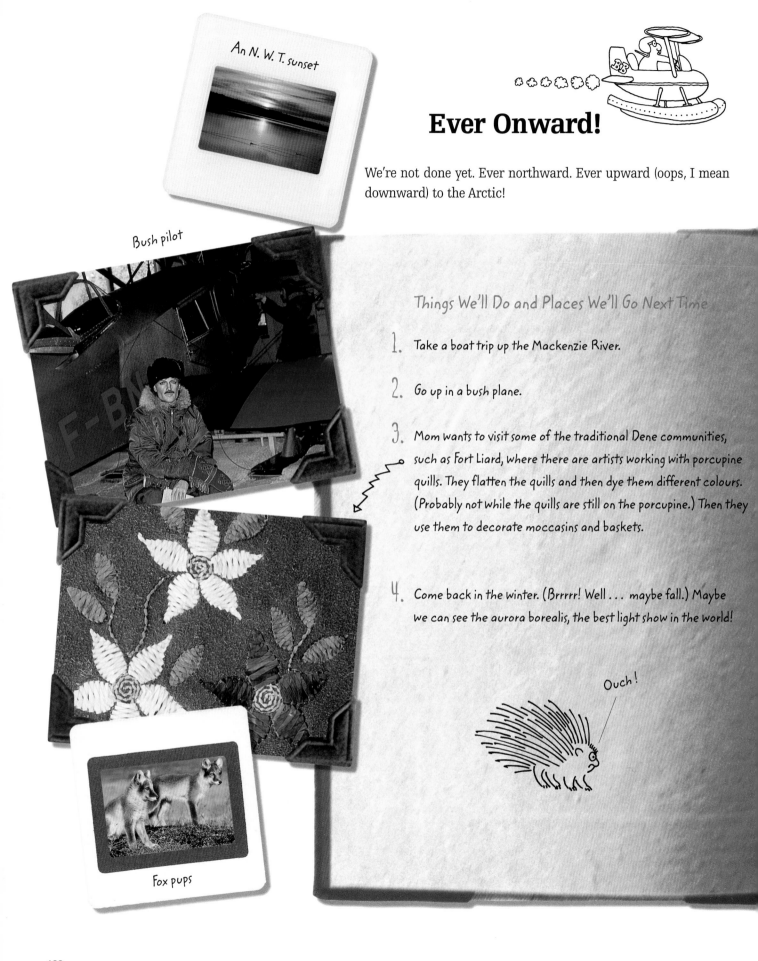

An N. W. T. sunset

Bush pilot

Fox pups

Ever Onward!

We're not done yet. Ever northward. Ever upward (oops, I mean downward) to the Arctic!

Things We'll Do and Places We'll Go Next Time

1. Take a boat trip up the Mackenzie River.

2. Go up in a bush plane.

3. Mom wants to visit some of the traditional Dene communities, such as Fort Liard, where there are artists working with porcupine quills. They flatten the quills and then dye them different colours. (Probably not while the quills are still on the porcupine.) Then they use them to decorate moccasins and baskets.

4. Come back in the winter. (Brrrrr! Well . . . maybe fall.) Maybe we can see the aurora borealis, the best light show in the world!

Ouch!

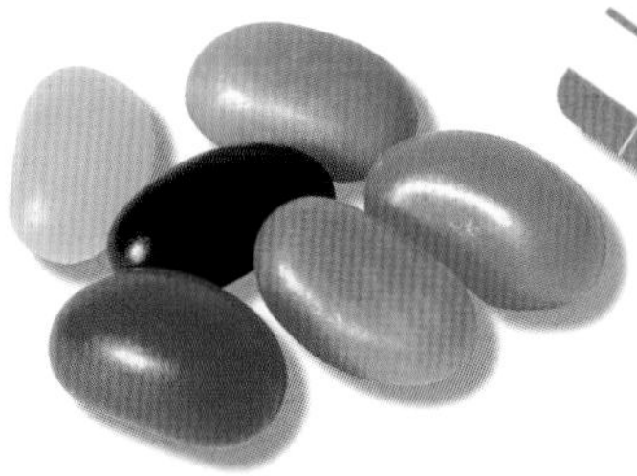

I think this rock might be gold.
(Guy says I'm a fool)

Found in Rachel's backpack

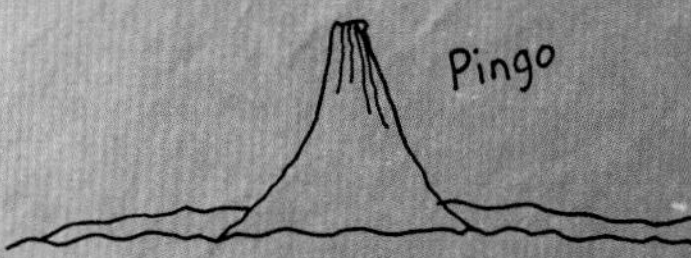

Pingo

5. Climb a pingo. A pingo is a volcano-shaped hill with a solid ice core. It's surrounded by a layer of permafrost. There are lots of pingos in the Mackenzie Delta area.

6. Take a rafting trip down the South Nahanni River and try to avoid plunging down Virginia Falls.

7. Visit one of the many mines in the N. W. T.

8. Visit Tuktoyaktuk (practice saying it first).

9. Visit Inuvik in early January to celebrate the first sunrise of the year.

10. Come to see the spring or fall caribou migration.

We're flying into Nunavut (noon-a-voot). Nunavut used to be part of Canada's Northwest Territories, but since April 1, 1999, it's a separate territory. Nunavut means "our land" in the Inuit language, Inuktitut, and it's where most of the Inuit live.

My goal is to see a kamgnimu. A what? Oh, sorry, I got it backwards. It's an umingmak. Umingmak means "the bearded one." It's the Inuit name for a muskox, a large beast with a shaggy skirt and long curving horns.

Territorial Flag

Territorial Arms

Provincial Flower
Purple Saxifrage

Magnetic North Pole

IT WANDERS. WAS LAST SEEN HERE.

NUNA

Victoria Island

Cambridge Bay

ALSO KNOWN A IQALUKTUUTIAG

Northwest Passage

Kugluktuk

Northwest Territories

Arctic Circle

Tree Line

Thelon River

Kazan Riv

Iqaluktuutiaq

(Cambridge Bay)

To: kheisler@relay.com
From: gbowers@galaxy.com
Subject: Halu, Kyle!

We're in Cambridge Bay, which is 300 km (186 miles) north of the Arctic Circle, on Victoria Island. Check it out on the map. In summer, it never gets dark at night. I guess because we're so far north, Rachel expected everything to be snow and ice, even in the summer. She can't believe that kids are riding on bicycles and playing on the playground. Even in the middle of the night!

There aren't many cars because there aren't many roads. Instead, everyone rides around on ATVs in summer and snowmobiles in winter. People live in regular houses with electricity, phones, televisions, and computers with Internet access. (You notice it didn't take me long to log on!)

There are two general stores that sell almost anything (including muskox and caribou meat). One even has a fast-food restaurant. Dad asked for *muktuk*, which he heard was an Inuit treat—rotting whale skin with a thin layer of fat. They laughed at him and gave him french fries instead. Mom almost choked when she saw the prices. You have to pay a lot for air-freighted potatoes.

No muskox in sight yet, but apparently we might see one tomorrow. We're going "out on the land," as they say here.

Later,
Guy

"Tuktusiuriagatigitqingnapinngitkyptinnga."
Our guidebook says that's the longest word in the
Invialuktun dialect of Inuktitut. It means
"You'll never go caribou hunting with me again."

136

According to Dad

Dad told us that fifty years ago the Inuit in this area were trappers and hunters. They lived in family groups on the land, following the animals. Now most of the Inuit of Cambridge Bay live in town in modern houses. Although many still go hunting, few use their traditional hunting and trapping skills to survive.

The Inuit we met here have kept some of their traditions, but at the same time they are part of the modern world. For instance, in Cambridge Bay we saw *komatiks* (traditional sleds) pulled by snowmobiles. We were offered bannock and french fries. And we met people wearing *amautiks* (traditional dress) and blue jeans.

According to Mom

English-speaking people used to call the Inuit "Eskimos." That's an insult! Mom read that *Eskimo* is a Cree word that has something to do with eating raw meat.

Inuit means "the people" in Inuktitut and, finally, people started calling them this! Incidentally, one Inuit is called an "*Inuk.*"

CERTIFICATE

Bear witness that

Guy Bowers

having demonstrated initiative, integrity and bold adventurous spirit of the true Arctic explorers who have crossed the Arctic Circle will hereafter be recognized as an honourable member of the exclusive Polar Bear Chapter, Order of Arctic Adventurers.

Here's my certificate for getting above the Arctic Circle.

The stop signs in Cambridge Bay are in both Inuktitut and English.

We took shelter from the wind inside some rings of piled rocks, which were apparently food caches used by the Inuit long ago.

Dad says the Arctic gets so little precipitation that it is really a polar desert. Figures. Only our family would go camping on a polar desert!

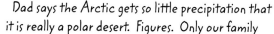

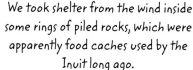

Guy's Wildlife List
Muskoxen

On the Land and in Cambridge Bay

The night before last, we camped out beside the Arctic Ocean. In the morning, I was still snuggled way down inside my sleeping bag when I heard Mom yell: "Muskoxen! I can see them from camp!"

Sure enough, away across the rolling tundra, some shaggy brown muskoxen were grazing on the grass. We spent all day tracking these hairy fellows across the tundra. We also watched Arctic terns dive-bombing for fish. These birds fly all the way from Antarctica to the Arctic every spring—and all the way back every fall. That's one long trip!

Now we're back in Cambridge Bay. We are getting to know lots of friendly people here, including a cool Husky dog called Alamo, which means "wolf" in Inuktitut. Inuktitut is taught in schools here. I learned how to say *koana* (pronounced ko-wana) which means "thank you." So now I can be polite in Inuktitut. My mother is ecstatic.

How to Make Arctic Tundra

1. Use a good-sized ice sheet to scrape the land down to bedrock. Scrape off all the soil. Spare no earthworms.

2. Water sparingly. (You are creating a polar desert, so hold the precipitation.)

A happy husky

This is an inuksuk, a stone structure built by the Inuit. Inuit have used them for hundreds of years to show direction and to help herd caribou during the hunt.

Eddie's son

This afternoon we went down to the harbour to see the Coast Guard ice-breaker. It travels in front of the supply barge, which should arrive here any day. The barge is towed all the way down the Mackenzie River from Hay River, on Great Slave Lake. It only comes once a year, so it's a big deal when it arrives. It brings in lumber, trucks, and anything else that is too big and heavy to send by plane.

On the dock we met a camera crew that is going on the Coast Guard ship to make a video of John Franklin's two sunken ships. Franklin was an Englishman who, in 1845, led an expedition looking for a way to sail from the Atlantic to the Pacific Ocean. He never returned. Over the next ten years, 32 other expeditions went looking for Franklin. They didn't find him, but they mapped a lot of the Arctic islands while they were looking. People now think Franklin and most of his expedition died on King William Island, and at Starvation Cove, east of here.

Food I Was Introduced to for My Own Good

A friend called Eddie and his son helped us fish for Arctic char. I don't like eating fish, but Mom said I should try some, since it's such a part of the local culture. "I've heard it's even better than macaroni and cheese," she joked. "Macaroni?" said Eddie, grinning. "I like it with wieners!" Now that's my kind of Inuit culture!

3. Keep your tundra in the deep freeze for most of the year. Allow to partially thaw every summer (enough to turn the ice into puddles, but not enough to let trees grow). Decorate with muskoxen and caribou. Sprinkle on mosquitoes.

Twelve Down, One to Go

Believe it or not, we only have one territory to go, and then we're finished our great Canadian adventure. Too bad—I was starting to like this travelling thing.

This is *qiviut* that I collected during our walk across the tundra. The muskoxen shed their inner coats in the spring, littering hair all over. Birds use it to build nests, and some people collect it for knitting.

Things We'll Do and Places We'll Go Next Time

1. Go even farther north and visit the High Arctic. (Who ever decided north was up?) Mom thinks Bylot Island would be great. I say we might as well go all the way up to Ellesmere Island, at the top of Canada. Rachel says why not go to the North Pole while we're at it. Dad says we had better win the lottery so we can pay for these plane trips to the High Arctic.

2. Visit Iqaluit, Nunavut's capital city, on Baffin Island.

3. Canoe the Thelon River through the Thelon Game Sanctuary. We'll see game (if we're game for it).

4. Somewhere, in the whole of Nunavut, there must be a mini-golf course we could visit next time. Wouldn't you think so? (Mom says she prefers not to think of such things.)

Polar bears

Our friend Christian, on the top of Mt. Pelly, near Cambridge Bay

LEMMINGS   LEMMINGS   LEMMINGS

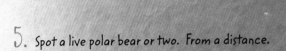

We're heading west to the Yukon. One more territory to go!

Exceedingly Weird

This is an Arctic telephone pole. You can't dig holes into the tundra (the ground is frozen down there, even in summer). So instead they hold up the poles with rocks, just like a Christmas tree.

5. Spot a live polar bear or two. From a distance.

6. Visit an old Thule Inuit site called Qaummaarviit, on an island at the head of Frobisher Bay. The Inuits' ancestors have lived in northern Canada for thousands of years. They are ancestors of the Thule people, who moved into this part of the Arctic about 1,000 years ago. Some of the remains of the Thule villages are still around.

7. Tour some of the territory's art studios, such as the ones in Cape Dorset, Baker Lake, and Rankin Inlet. See the soapstone carvings, some printmaking, and fabric wallhangings, and maybe meet some of the artists.

8. Go on a dog-team tour (but maybe not in the middle of winter, because we wouldn't see too much). Rachel thinks a snowmobile would get there faster. Dad said it would be noisier. I guess it depends on the dogs.

Arctic cotton—dead.
It was growing outside our tent. The Inuit used to use it as a wick for their soapstone lamps and stoves. The lamps burned seal blubber, fish oil, or caribou fat. These days, the Inuit use microwave ovens.

Arctic cotton—alive

141

Yukon, ho! We're off to the Klondike to find gold! (That is a very Yukon-ish thing to do.) We'll be meeting friends and we'll spend five days canoeing with them down the Yukon River to the gold fields.

"After we strike it rich, let's blow all our money in the saloons and dance halls of Dawson City like the people who came here during the Klondike Gold Rush," says Mom.

"Can't I save some and spend it responsibly?" I ask.

"Not allowed."

Yukon is the last territory we'll visit. This is astounding!

Ready for Yukon? Mush!

Territorial Flower Fireweed

Territorial Flag

Territorial Arms

To the Klondike by Land

"Not Chilkoot Pass," I said, panicking. "I've heard of Chilkoot Pass. I'll never make it up! I'll collapse in a pathetic heap! I'll . . ."

". . . take the train," said Mom.

Train? Did I hear train? Phew!

Chilkoot Pass is the mountain pass that thousands of gold-seekers hauled lots of gear over to get to the Yukon during the Klondike Gold Rush over a hundred years ago. Long strings of miners, laden down with packs, trudged single file up a never-ending slope. Today, that same Klondike trail has become a popular five-day hike for people who actually like unnecessary suffering.

Lucky for us, someone thought of building a train track along a parallel route through the mountains and over White Pass. The White Pass & Yukon Route Railway still carries passengers along this route from Skagway on the Alaskan coast to Bennett Lake in the Yukon. It's one of the steepest railways in North America, climbing 873 m (2,865 ft.) in just 32 km (20 miles), with a few cliff-hanging turns thrown in for good measure. What a view!

They said it couldn't be done, but in 1898, construction began on the WP&YR Railway. Fighting fierce snowstorms, cold weather, and very dangerous conditions, railway workers blasted tunnels and laid a track through the mountains in just over two years.

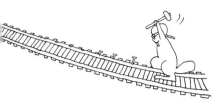

We got off the train at Bennett Lake. It's from here that, during the Klondike Gold Rush, miners piled their year's worth of supplies onto rafts or boats and drifted (or drowned!) their way down icy rivers and killer rapids on the harrowing 885 km (550 mile) journey to the gold fields. It was treacherous—but I guess people thought it was worth it. They were gold crazy!

We decided to do our journey by car instead of boat. Back in Whitehorse, we checked out the S. S. *Klondike*, the biggest of the sternwheelers that cruised down the Yukon River to Dawson City before they built the highway that people now use instead. The ship has been turned into a museum.

Then we went to a log church, which is the oldest building in Whitehorse, and learned about "The Bishop Who Ate His Boots." Apparently a Yukon bishop got lost in ice fog when it was way, way below freezing. He was starving, so he boiled up his sealskin and walrus-soled boots and drank the broth.

"I wonder what my sneakers would taste like boiled," said Rachel.

"Let's just make sure we don't get lost," said Dad.

According to Mom

The Alaska Highway is how most people drive into Yukon from southern Canada. The highway continues on to Alaska. It was built in a big rush in 1942 (there's lots of rushing in this territory). For eight months, soldiers worked day and night, seven days a week. Floods tore out bridges. Bogs swallowed up heavy equipment. Workers got frostbite in cold weather, or were eaten alive by bugs when it warmed up.

Some people today call the highway the "Alcan Highway." (Get it? "Al" for Alaska and "Can" for Canada.) Some people call it the "Oil Can Highway."

How to Make a Sternwheeler Go

1. Burn wood (lots of wood) to heat water in the boiler. The ships gobbled up so much wood, the crew had to stop frequently to load up with more (there are remains of these refuelling stations along the Yukon River).

2. The hot boiler produces steam.

3. The steam powers huge pistons that turn the sternwheel.

4. The turning of the water wheel makes the ship move.

The sternwheelers were made with a shallow draft so they could cruise the shallow channels of the Yukon River without running aground.

In the sternwheeler cabin

To the Klondike by River

I'm in a canoe in the middle of the Yukon River. I'm in Fred's canoe, and my cousin Joel is paddling in the bow. If he doesn't accidentally splash me—or, more likely, splash me on purpose—and if Rachel doesn't squirt me with her water pistol (she still owes me one from our water fight this morning), I should be able to keep this page dry. Place your bets?

Our three canoes are floating north to Dawson City, just like the gold-seekers did in 1898. Except they paddled through murderous rapids, suffered numbing cold, and practically died on the way. We're avoiding most of the nasty stuff. We're not avoiding the nasty mosquitoes, though. Joel has so many bites, he looks like he has some terrible disease.

Every night we camp on a sandbar or an island in the river. I go to sleep listening to the river gurgling and Dad snoring (they're definitely not in harmony). The first night, a raven swooped down and swiped all the sausage meat that was supposed to be our dinner. Yukon ravens are huge and smart—and they have no manners!

We explore abandoned settlements and old steamboat-refuelling stops along the river. The old cabins along the river are overgrown with purple fireweed flowers and feel like . . . well, there just might be ghosts around. We peek in windows and see old brass bedsteads and home-made tables and chairs. Joel found a perfectly good rubber boot, which he is keeping in case we find the other one.

Hey, I have an idea!

"Joel! Instead of looking for your other boot, why don't we just get rid of one of your feet?"

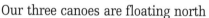

Darn it! Now my page is soaked!

Exceedingly Weird

Weird and Wonderful Mosquitoes

Fred shared his mosquito knowledge with me. Did you know:

1. Only female mosquitoes bite.

2. Mosquitoes don't actually suck blood out of you. They use a pump in their heads. It works sort of the way a turkey baster does to suck up fat from the pan.

3. Mosquitoes keep slurping in blood until a signal from their stretched abdomen tells the brain to quit. In experiments where these nerves to the brain were cut, the mosquitoes kept on pumping in blood until they burst.

4. It would take about 1,120,000 mosquito bites to drain all the blood from an average person (I think Joel might be getting close).

5. A mosquito's brain is the size of the period at the end of this sentence.

Guy's Wildlife List
Grizzly bear

Guy's Wildlife List
Bald eagle

Guy's Wildlife List
Lynx

Yesterday was the best wildlife day yet! First, we saw two moose. They raised their heads out of the water, plants hanging out of their mouths, and stared at us as we swept by. They didn't seem as excited to see us as we were to spot them. We also saw at least two bald eagles, a grizzly in the distance, and—the best sighting of the day—a lynx, standing motionless near the river. It looked like an exceedingly large house cat. It saw us, but it didn't move. We all stopped paddling and drifted by. We watched the lynx and it watched us, until we rounded a bend and couldn't see it anymore. Wow!

I also caught a fish! I got the bite just as we were negotiating a tricky stretch of river where it sweeps around a bend between high clay cliffs. Great excitement and instant chaos! Fred got all flustered trying to paddle and hold the fish net at the same time, Joel tried to brace the canoe as it slowly twirled in the current, people in the other canoes shouted, and my fish thrashed and tugged. Anyway, we now have a 20 cm (8 in.) arctic grayling, which we'll have with supper.

Food I Was Introduced to for My Own Good

Our friend Sue decided we should eat like the stampeding miners did. She brought some sourdough starter with her so we could have sourdough flapjacks for breakfast. Sourdough starter is a spongy goop of flour, water, and yeast. The miners used to take it to bed with them and keep it beside their bodies because it was no good if it froze. That's why Yukon old-timers are sometimes called "sourdoughs." It tastes a lot better than it looks. Guess whose turn it is tonight to sleep with a jar of sourdough? Sue promises it won't leak.

Guy's Family Canoe Trip Survival Tips

Here are some things to do in a canoe when you're not paddling.

1. Squirt the occupants of the other canoes with water pistols. (Be prepared for retaliation.)
2. Have drag races.
3. Watch out for shallows and sandbars so you don't run aground.
4. Watch swooping swallows (they nest high up on the cliffs).
5. Catch fish.
6. Sing songs.
7. Yell insults.

147

Gold nuggets!

Dawson City

According to Dad

How to Pan for Gold

1. Keep your shirt buttoned up so you won't lose it.

2. Scoop up creek gravel and water in your gold pan.

3. Slosh the water around in circles in the pan so that the gold and other heavy bits sink to the bottom but the lighter bits spill off the top.

4. Keep doing this with more and more gravel and water. (Is your shirt still on? Good!)

5. Sort through the heavy stones that have sunk to the bottom. Pick out the gold nuggets. Discard the marbles and fishing sinkers.

6. Take the gold to the bank and cash it in. Go on a wild spending spree! Spend all your money! End up penniless. (At least you didn't lose your shirt.)

We paddled into Dawson City, past enormous piles of gravel at the sides of the river. They were left by the dredging machines. The early miners used shovels and gold pans to find gold. Later, huge dredges tore up the creekbed looking for whatever the early miners missed. I wonder how many fish survived the Klondike Gold Rush?

We drove to see enormous Dredge No. 4, which is now a tourist attraction. It's the largest such dredge in North America— a gargantuan monster machine eight-storeys high that covers an area almost the size of a football field.

We got here a hundred years too late for the actual Klondike Gold Rush, but things haven't changed all that much in Dawson City. It still looks like 1898. Some people haven't even changed their clothes. When you walk along the boardwalk, it feels like you're in a western movie. The old buildings have fancy fronts, but if you look around the back you can see they're false fronts stuck onto plain buildings.

You can still gamble away your money and watch the can-can girls dance at Diamond Tooth Gertie's. You can see a show at the Palace Grand Theatre, booing and hissing the villains and cheering the red-coated Mounties when they come to the rescue.

148

Dredge No. 4

The Palace Grand

People in period costume
at the post office

The can-can at the
Red Theatre Saloon

While eating lunch at Klondike Kate's, we met some mountaineers who had just climbed Mount Logan—the highest mountain in Canada. It's in Kluane National Park. These guys flew in a small plane to the glacier at the base of the mountain, and took almost three weeks to do the climb. They had sunburnt faces from the sun reflected off the snow, and white "owl eyes" from their sunglasses.

"Wow, I bet you're tired," said Rachel.

"Hungry," said one of them. "I lost almost 4 kg (9 lbs) on the climb, and I've been pigging out ever since I got down. Say, what's that you're eating? It looks good!"

Tomorrow, we're going to Bonanza Creek to pan for gold. I'm going to strike it rich!

"Not to discourage you," said Mom, "but most gold-seekers in the Klondike lost their shirts. They didn't find gold. Their mining claims were worthless."

I'll bet they just didn't know where to look for the gold. Just you wait. There's gold in that creek, and I'm going to find it!

P.S. (Next day) Drat!

According to Mom

It all began when George Carmacks, Skookum Jim, and Dawson Charlie struck gold on Bonanza Creek (near Dawson City) in 1896. Word got out, and the stampede was on! What a crazy time it must have been, with saloons going night and day, dance halls and gambling establishments booming, gold dust and whiskey flowing, and fortunes won and lost. The boom didn't last more than a few years. Soon, the mines that could be easily worked were all finished. Dredges continued to chew up the creekbeds and extract gold, but most gold-seekers went rushing off to the next gold rush.

BUCKO BEAVER RAMS HIS SUPER-POWERED TIME-TRAVELLING GIZMO INTO REVERSE. NOT FAR TO GO. HE SCREECHES TO A HALT IN 1898. STEPPING OUT OF HIS MACHINE, HE IS HIT HARD BY A HERD OF STAMPEDING MINERS! HEY—WHAT'S THE BIG RUSH?

OUR ROUGHED-UP RODENT HEADS INTO TOWN TO RECOVER. HE FINDS A DENTIST WILLING TO REPLACE HIS CHIPPED BUCK TOOTH WITH A DIAMOND VERSION. DIAMOND-TOOTHED BUCKO HITS THE DANCE HALL STAGE, SHOWING THAT HE CAN INDEED CAN-CAN WITH THE BEST OF THEM!

What's Next?

Surely the trip can't be over. We've *only* seen ten provinces and three territories. I keep thinking my parents are going to find another Canadian province or territory that they somehow forgot to tell us about. I just thought we'd keep travelling forever.

Things We'll Do and Places We'll Go Next Time

1. We'll drive north up the Dempster Highway, through the Richardson Mountains, to Tuktoyaktuk and Inuvik on the Arctic Ocean.

2. We'll come to Whitehorse in February for the Yukon Sourdough Rendezvous Festival. We'll watch flour-packing and chainsaw-chucking contests.

3. We'll visit Kluane National Park to hike (well, some of us), see Dall's sheep on Sheep Mountain, and see 18,000-year-old mammoth tusks at the Kluane Museum of Natural History at Burwash Landing.

4. Mom thinks I'll surprise everyone and hike the Chilkoot Trail to the Yukon some day. That sure would surprise me! She says that one day I'll probably be a really keen hiker and she'll kid me about the old days when I hated it. Dream on, Mom.

Rachel says she'll come back in ten years to climb Mount Logan, the tallest mountain in Canada.

Part of Mount Logan known as the diving board

The traverse, Mount Logan

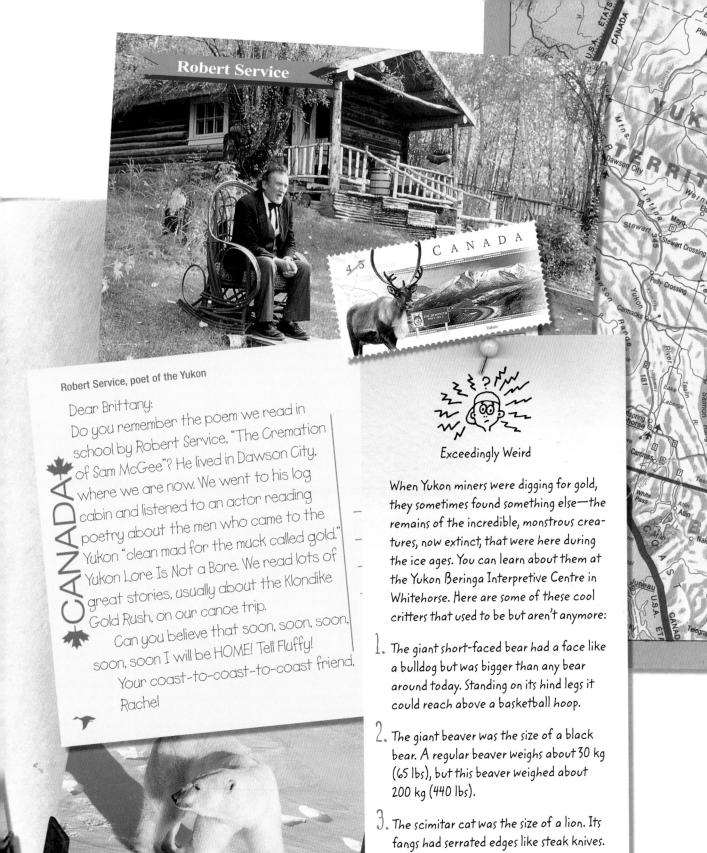

Robert Service

Robert Service, poet of the Yukon

CANADA

Dear Brittany:

Do you remember the poem we read in school by Robert Service, "The Cremation of Sam McGee"? He lived in Dawson City, where we are now. We went to his log cabin and listened to an actor reading poetry about the men who came to the Yukon "clean mad for the muck called gold." Yukon Lore Is Not a Bore. We read lots of great stories, usually about the Klondike Gold Rush, on our canoe trip.

Can you believe that soon, soon, soon, soon, soon I will be HOME! Tell Fluffy!

Your coast-to-coast-to-coast friend,

Rachel

I HAVE to come back to the Far North because I haven't seen a polar bear yet!

Exceedingly Weird

When Yukon miners were digging for gold, they sometimes found something else—the remains of the incredible, monstrous creatures, now extinct, that were here during the ice ages. You can learn about them at the Yukon Beringia Interpretive Centre in Whitehorse. Here are some of these cool critters that used to be but aren't anymore:

1. The giant short-faced bear had a face like a bulldog but was bigger than any bear around today. Standing on its hind legs it could reach above a basketball hoop.

2. The giant beaver was the size of a black bear. A regular beaver weighs about 30 kg (65 lbs), but this beaver weighed about 200 kg (440 lbs).

3. The scimitar cat was the size of a lion. Its fangs had serrated edges like steak knives.

4. And the most fearsome of all: the giant Rachel. It was 3 m (10 ft.) tall, with yellow hair and an annoying need to always be singing.

Rachel's backpack and Bucko Beaver AFTER the trip . . .

CAMPFIRE CHAT

We Did It!

We're on our way home. I can't quite believe it. Mom and Dad promise this really is our last night on the road before we can sleep in our own beds. We're celebrating our last camp cookout with a meal of hotdogs cooked over the fire. Yum!

"What was your favourite part of the whole trip?" asked Dad, as I polished off my fourth hotdog.

"Are you kidding?" said Rachel. "It was so long, I can't even remember most of the trip!"

"Oh, great," said Mom. "I'm glad we took the time to show it all to you."

"I thought we did way too much driving," I said. "But I liked the wildlife. Especially that lynx we saw on the Yukon River. And muskoxen in Nunavut. I liked the whales in the Maritimes, and the gannet colony in Gaspésie."

"What about icebergs?" said Rachel. "Remember that big one we saw—where was it?"

"Try Newfoundland," I suggested.

"That's right! Those icebergs were cool!" said Rachel.

"Downright chilly," said Dad.

"Remember looking for dinosaur fossils in Alberta?" said Mom.

"Yeah, and Guy almost ate fossilized dinosaur dung!" said Rachel.

"I did not!"

"I'll bet Guy remembers that wonderful hike up to the glacier in B.C." said Dad.

"When I almost died."

"I had no idea!" said Mom.

"Remember how Mom kept getting mixed up every time she came out of the subway in Toronto?"

"And Dad wouldn't stand on the glass floor at the top of the CN Tower?"

"What about the historical places?" asked Mom. "Like Louisbourg."

"Louisbourg was cool!" said Rachel.

"The Viking place in Newfoundland was good," I said. "I liked wearing that helmet and sword."

"You liked Head-Smashed-In Buffalo Jump, didn't you? And Quebec City?" she reminded me.

"Yeah. I guess the historical stuff was okay, after all."

"So," said Mom, "do you figure you learned a thing or two about Canada?"

"No way!" said Rachel. "This trip wasn't supposed to be educational, right?"

Yeah, right.

"What do you think, Guy?" asked Mom.

"I think that when I get home, I would like to have the first bath," I said.

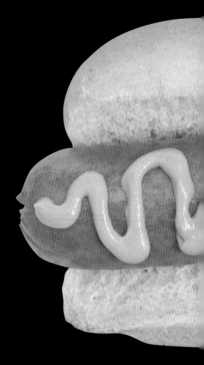

It's the Facts!

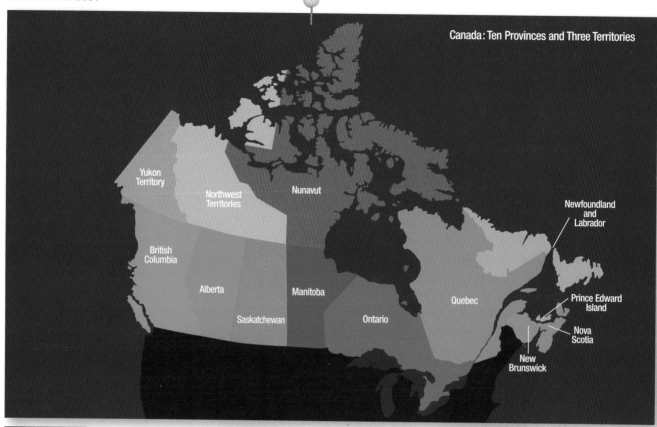

Canada: Ten Provinces and Three Territories

 Canada

National Symbols

Arms   Animal: Beaver   Tree: Maple Tree

Origin of the name: Likely from the Huron-Iroquois word *kanata*, meaning "village" or "small community," referring to the area along the St. Lawrence River.

Size: 9,970,610 sq. km (3,849,955 sq. miles)

Population: 33,311,400

Capital city: Ottawa

Other major cities: Toronto, Montreal, Vancouver, Calgary

Major industries: Agriculture, forestry, mining

Official Web page: www.canada.gc.ca

Snapshot: Canada is the second-largest country in the world, but it does not have a big population (Tokyo, Japan, has almost as many people living in it and its surrounding area as in all of Canada!). Nearly 90% of Canada's population lives along its southern border (with the United States). Canada is made up of ten provinces and three territories in the north. The country has two official languages, English and French.

 British Columbia

Origin of the name: The southern part of the province was named "Columbia" after the river running through it. The "British" part was added to the name to avoid confusion with Colombia, a country in South America.

Provincial Symbols
  Bird: Steller's Jay
  Flower: Pacific Dogwood
  Tree: Western Red Cedar

Size: 947,800 sq. km (365,975 sq. miles)

Population: 4,381,600

Capital city: Victoria

Other major cities: Vancouver, Prince George, Kamloops, Kelowna

Major industries: Forestry (lumber, pulp and paper, newsprint, shingles and shakes), tourism, mining, fishing, agriculture

Web page: www.gov.bc.ca

Snapshot: B.C. is a province of contrasts, from the Pacific coastline to high mountain ranges inland to flat prairie grasslands in the northeast corner. The climate and vegetation are similarly varied. The coast has a mild, wet climate, while parts of the interior are much drier—even desert! Much of the province is mountainous and forested; B.C. produces one-half of Canada's lumber. Most people live along the coast or in the mountain valleys, especially around Vancouver and Victoria.

 Alberta

Origin of the name: Named for Queen Victoria's fourth daughter, Princess Louise Caroline Alberta, the wife of the Governor General of Canada when the province was formed in 1882.

Provincial Symbols
  Bird: Great Horned Owl
  Flower: Wild Rose
  Tree: Lodgepole Pine

Size: 661,190 sq. km (255,305 sq. miles)

Population: 3,585,100

Capital city: Edmonton

Other major cities: Calgary, Lethbridge, Red Deer

Major industries: Energy, agriculture (wheat, livestock), forestry, tourism, and advanced technology.

Web page: www.gov.ab.ca

Snapshot: Alberta is a prairie province, bordered by the Rocky Mountains and foothills on the west. The southern part of Alberta is mostly flat, with fields of grain. The north has rivers, lakes, forests, and muskeg. Alberta gets more sun than any other province. Drilling for oil and natural gas has made the province wealthy, but grain farming and ranching are also important.

Saskatchewan

Origin of the name: From the Cree name for the Saskatchewan River, *kisiskatchanisipi*, meaning "swift current."
Provincial Symbols
  Bird: Prairie Sharp-tailed Grouse
  Flower: Western Red Lily
  Tree: White Birch
Size: 652,330 sq. km (251,884 sq. miles)
Population: 1,016,000
Capital city: Regina
Other major cities: Saskatoon, Prince Albert, Moose Jaw
Major industries: Agriculture (wheat, canola), forestry, mining (potash, uranium, coal, oil and natural gas)
Web page: www.gov.sk.ca
Snapshot: This flat prairie province is one of the world's greatest producers of wheat and grows two-thirds of Canada's supply. Part of the Canadian Shield, Northern Saskatchewan is covered in forests, lakes, rivers, and bogs. The province is the world's leading exporter of potash, a mineral used as fertilizer for crops. Summers are hot (the hottest temperature ever recorded in Canada—45°C [113°F]—was in Saskatchewan) and winters are cold.

Manitoba

Origin of the name: Likely from the Cree *Manitou bah,* meaning "the narrows of the Great Spirit." This refers to a narrow part of Lake Manitoba where waves on the rocks make a bell-like and wailing sound, thought to be the sound of the spirit Manitou beating a drum.
Provincial Symbols
  Bird: Great Gray Owl
  Flower: Prairie Crocus
  Tree: White Spruce
Size: 649,950 sq. km (250,965 sq. miles)
Population: 1,208,000
Capital city: Winnipeg
Other major cities: Brandon, Portage la Prairie, Thompson
Major industries: Manufacturing (food, transportation equipment), agriculture (wheat and other grains, cattle), mining (nickel, copper, zinc)
Web page: www.gov.mb.ca
Snapshot: Sunny Manitoba is sometimes called the Land of 100,000 Lakes. The southern half of Manitoba is prairie, while the northern part is rocky, hilly Canadian Shield covered with forest. Manitoba summers are hot, and the winters are cold.

Manitobans have many different ethnic and cultural origins. The province has large populations of Mennonites, Ukrainians, and the largest French-speaking community in western Canada. First Nations (especially Cree, Assiniboine) make up about 7% of the population. More than half the population of Manitoba lives in Winnipeg.

Ontario

Origin of the name: From the Iroquois word *kanadario,* meaning "sparkling water."
Provincial Symbols
  Bird: Common Loon
  Flower: White Trillium
  Tree: Eastern White Pine
Size: 1,068,580 sq. km (412,610 sq. miles)
Population: 12,929,000
Capital city: Toronto
Other major cities: Ottawa, Kingston, London, Thunder Bay, Sudbury, Sault Ste. Marie, Hamilton
Major industries: Manufacturing (automobiles), mining (gold, nickel, copper, uranium, zinc), forestry, financial industries, tourism
Web page: www.gov.on.ca
Snapshot: Canada's second-largest province and the one with the most people, Ontario has three main regions: the wet, scrubby lowlands around Hudson Bay; the rocky Canadian Shield of Northern Ontario; and the lowlands around the Great Lakes and St. Lawrence River in the south (where most of the province's population and industry is). Southern Ontario's mild climate and fertile soil make it an important agricultural area. Toronto is the headquarters for many Canadian businesses; Ottawa is the national capital; and Niagara Falls is one of Canada's major tourist attractions.

Quebec

Origin of the name: From the Algonquin word *quebecq* for "narrow passage" or "strait," referring to the narrow part of the St. Lawrence River at Quebec City.
Provincial Symbols
  Bird: Snowy Owl
  Flower: Blue Flag
  Tree: Yellow Birch
Size: 1,540,680 sq. km (594,903 sq. miles)
Population: 7,750,500
Capital city: Quebec City
Other major cities: Montreal, Trois-Rivières, Laval, Sherbrooke

Major industries: Manufacturing (paper), hydroelectric generation (on James Bay), agriculture, mining (aluminum, iron ore), forestry
Web page: www.gouv.qc.ca (you can click on the "English" link at the bottom of the page)
Snapshot: Quebec is Canada's largest province. The north is part of the Canadian Shield, and the Appalachian Mountains are along the southern border. In between, where you'll find most of the people and the cities, are the lowlands of the St. Lawrence River. The official language in Quebec is French, and 83% of Quebecois have French as their mother tongue. The province's culture (laws, customs, music, food) is quite different from that found elsewhere in the country. There has been ongoing debate about the idea of Quebec separating from the rest of Canada, but so far the majority of the population has always voted "no" to this.

Prince Edward Island

Origin of the name: Named to honour the son of King George III of England, Prince Edward.
Provincial Symbols
  Bird: Blue Jay
  Flower: Lady's Slipper
  Tree: Red Oak
Size: 5,660 sq. km (2,185 sq. miles)
Population: 139,800
Capital city: Charlottetown
Major industries: Agriculture (potatoes), tourism, fishing
Web page: www.gov.pe.ca
Snapshot: Canada's smallest province, one of the Maritime provinces, PEI is mostly gently rolling farmland. It's known for its potatoes, which grow well in the rich, red soil and mild climate. Many tourists visit Green Gables, home of the fictional character in the novel *Anne of Green Gables.*

New Brunswick

Origin of the name: Named to honour King George III of England, who was also the Duke of Brunswick.
Provincial Symbols
  Bird: Black-capped Chickadee
  Flower: Purple Violet
  Tree: Balsam Fir
Size: 73,440 sq. km (28,357 sq. miles)
Population: 747,300
Capital city: Fredericton
Other major cities: Saint John, Moncton

Major industries: Forestry (pulp and paper), manufacturing (food and drink products), mining, tourism, fishing, agriculture

Web page: www.gov.nb.ca

Snapshot: New Brunswick is one of the Maritime provinces. It's 85% forested, with mountains in the north and rolling farmland along the Saint John River Valley. It's Canada's only officially bilingual province, and many people speak French or have French ancestors.

 Nova Scotia

Origin of the name: "Nova Scotia" is Latin for "New Scotland." It was named by Sir William Alexander, who received a grant to the land from King James VI of Scotland.

Provincial Symbols
  Bird: Osprey
  Flower: Mayflower
  Tree: Red Spruce

Size: 55,490 sq. km (21,425 sq. miles)

Population: 938,300

Capital city: Halifax

Other major cities: Sydney

Major industries: Manufacturing, agriculture (dairy), fishing, mining (coal), ship building, tourism

Web page: www.gov.ns.ca

Snapshot: One of the Maritime provinces, Nova Scotia is surrounded by water. Fishing villages dot the bays and inlets along the coast. Inland, the province is mostly forested, although the Annapolis Valley is scenic farm country known for its apples. Rugged and mountainous Cape Breton Island lies at the north end of the province. About 80% of the population is of English, Scottish, or Irish descent.

 Newfoundland and Labrador

Origin of the name: From "New Found Launde," which is what King Henry VII of England called the land discovered by John Cabot in 1497. Labrador was named by the Portuguese explorer João Fernandes, who was a *lavrador*, or landowner.

Provincial Symbols
  Bird: Atlantic Puffin
  Flower: Pitcher Plant
  Tree: Black Spruce

Size: 405,720 sq. km (156,660 sq. miles)

Population: 507,900

Capital city: St. John's

Other major cities: Grand Falls, Windsor, Corner Brook

Major industries: Fishing, mining (nickel, oil and natural gas), forestry (newsprint)

Web page: www.gov.nf.ca

Snapshot: This province is made up of two quite different parts—the island of Newfoundland (nicknamed "The Rock") and the mainland region of Labrador. Most of the population lives along the coast of Newfoundland. For years their traditional way of life was based on fishing, especially for cod. A ban on cod fishing put many out of work. Labrador is inhabited by Inuit, with smaller numbers of Innu Native people. The interior of both Newfoundland and Labrador is mainly forested, with countless lakes, rivers, and peat bogs. Northern Labrador has no trees; the Torngat Mountains dominate the landscape.

 Northwest Territories

Origin of the name: This area was earlier known as the North-West Territory because it was (you guessed it!) in the north and west part of the continent.

Territorial Symbols
  Bird: Gyrfalcon
  Flower: Mountain Avens
  Tree: Tamarack

Size: 1,432,320 sq. km (553,062 sq. miles)

Population: 43,300

Capital city: Yellowknife

Other major cities: Inuvik

Major industries: Mining (zinc, gold, diamonds), oil and gas exploration, tourism

Web page: www.gov.nt.ca

Snapshot: N. W. T. covers a huge area. The southern part of the territory is in the taiga zone, an area covered with short, coniferous forests. Farther north are the vast, treeless plains of the tundra, dotted with hundreds of lakes and rivers. The Mackenzie Mountains lie along the Yukon border to the west. The climate is dry, with long, cold winters, and summers that can be quite warm, at least in the south. About half the population is Native peoples, such as the Dene, Inuvialuit, and Métis. Eight official languages are used in the N. W. T. Legislative Assembly (where government representatives meet) in Yellowknife: Chipewyan, Cree, Dogrib, English, French, Gwitch'in, Inuktitut, and Slavey.

 Nunavut

Origin of the name: Means "our land" in Inuktitut, the Inuit language.

Territorial Symbols
  Bird: Rock Ptarmigan
  Flower: Purple Saxifrage
  Other: Canadian Inuit Dog

Size: 1,994,000 sq. km (769,945 sq. miles)

Population: 31,400

Capital city: Iqaluit

Major industries: Mining, tourism

Web page: www.gov.nu.ca

Snapshot: Canada's newest territory was formed April 1, 1999. Before that, it was part of the Northwest Territories. Like N. W. T., the southern part of Nunavut has the short, coniferous forests of the taiga, while the northern landscape is treeless tundra. Even in summer, when flowers bloom on the tundra, there is a layer of permafrost not far below. Nunavut includes Arctic islands stretching up to the North Pole. This is the land of the midnight sun in summer, as well as long, dark winters with little sunlight. The small population of Nunavut is largely Inuit. There are three official languages: English, French, and Inuktitut. Inuktitut is the working language of the government. Nunavut's system of government combines traditional Inuit ways with modern government systems.

 Yukon Territory

Origin of the name: Likely from the word *yukunah* in the Gwitch'in language or the Loucheux Indian word *yuchoo*, both meaning "great river" (referring to the Yukon River).

Territorial Symbols
  Bird: Raven
  Flower: Fireweed
  Tree: Sub-Alpine Fir

Size: 483,450 sq. km (186,675 sq. miles)

Population: 33,100

Capital city: Whitehorse

Major industries: Mining (gold, lead, zinc), tourism

Web page: www.gov.yk.ca

Snapshot: Triangular-shaped Yukon is almost entirely covered by mountain ranges. Mount Logan, Canada's highest mountain, at 5,951 m (19,525 ft.), is in the St. Elias Mountain Range in the southwest corner of the territory. The landscape of the southern part of the territory is taiga, with short, coniferous forests, while the north is tundra. Summers are short and warm (even hot!); winters are long and cold. Two-thirds of the population lives in the area around Whitehorse, the capital.

Index

Page numbers in italics refer to photographs and captions

A

Acadian Coast, 92–93
Acadians, explusion of, 92, *102*
Agassiz, Lake, 48
Alaska Highway, 19, 145
ALBERTA, 20–29
Alberta Provincial Museum, 28
Albertosaurus, 27
Alexander Graham Bell Museum, 109
Algonquin peoples, 67, 74
American kestrel, 26
Amethyst, *54*, 110
Annapolis Royal (N.S.), 102
Anne of Green Gables, *89*
L'Anse aux Meadows (Nfld.), 120
Antarctica, 138
Anthem, national, 75
Antigonish (N.S.), 110
Arctic char, 139
Arctic Circle, 136
Arctic cotton, *141*
Arctic tern, 138
Arms, provincial:
  Alberta, 20
  British Columbia, 6
  Manitoba, 42
  New Brunswick, 90
  Newfoudland, 112
  Nova Scotia, 100
  Ontario, 52
  PEI, 84
  Quebec, 68
  Saskatchewan, 32
Arms, territorial:
  Northwest Territories, 126
  Nunavut, 134
  Yukon, 142
Assiniboine Park, *51*
Assiniboine River, 47
Athabasca Glacier, 28
Athabasca Sand Dunes Provincial Park, 40
Atlantic salmon, 81
Aurora borealis, 132
Avalanches, 17

B

Baddeck (N.S.), 109
Baffin Island, 140
Baker Lake, 141
Balancing Rock (N.S.), 103
Bald eagle, 147, *147*
Banana slugs, 11
Banff National Park, 29
Bannock, 131, 137
Basilica of Saint Boniface, *46*, 47
Batoche National Historic Site, 41, *41*
Battlefields National Park, *74*, 75
Bay of Chaleurs, 92
Bears: great, short-faced, 151;
  grizzly, 14, 147, *147*; polar, 50, *126*,
  131, *140*
Beaver, giant, 151
Bell, Alexander Graham, 109
Bell Island (Nfld.), 115
Beluga whales, 73
Beothuks, 118
Bilingualism, 68, 82-83
Biodôme, 72–73, *72*, *73*
Bird sanctuaries, 26, 78, *79*, 122
Birds, migration, *34*, 66, 138
Bison, 36, 39, 50, 126–27, *126*, *127*
Blackfoot people, 24, 31
Bluenose II, 104
Bonanza Creek (Yukon), 149
Bonavista (Nfld.), 117, 122
BRITISH COLUMBIA, 6-19
Buffalo, 24, *24*
Burrowing owls, *26*
Bylot Island, 140

C

Cabot, John, 117, 122
Calgary, 22–23
Calgary Stampede, *22*
Cambridge Bay (Nun.), 136–37, *136*,
  138–39
Canadian Shield, 42
Canadian Snowbirds, 38, 41, *42*
Canadian War Museum, 65
Cape Breton Highlands, *111*
Cape Breton Island, 106, 108, 117
Cape Dorset, 141
Cape Enrage (N.B.), 98
Cape Spear (Nfld.), *115*
Capelin, 116, *116*
Cape May warbler, *66*
Cap-Tourmente National Wildlife Area, 81
Caribana, 61
Caribou migration, *133*
Carmacks, George, 149
Cat village (Ottawa), *67*
Ceilidh, 110
Champlain, Samuel de, 66, 74, 102
Charlottetown (PEI), 86–87
Chief Poundmaker Memorial Powwow, 40
Chignecto Bay (N.B.), 98
Chilkoot Pass (Yukon), 144
Chilkoot Trail, 150
Chinatown(s), 13, *13*, 61
Chinese language, 13
Chinook, 25
Churchill (Man.), 50
Churchill River, 40
Cirque du Soleil, 71
Citadel (Halifax), 104, *104*
Clearwater River, 40
CN Tower, 58-59, *58*, *59*
Coal mining, 108–109
Cobequid Bay (N.S.), 110
Cod fishing, 102, 107, 116
Columbia Icefield, 28
Columbia River, 16
Columbus, Christopher, 117
Common terns, 93
Confederation Bridge, 84
Confederation, Fathers of, 86
Coprolite, 27
Cree, 30, 31, 39
Cypress Hills, 34–35, *34*
Cut Knife (Sask.), 40

D

Dams, 16
Dawson Charlie, 149
Dawson City (Yukon), 142, 145,
  146, 148–49, 151
Dene people, 128, 130, *130*, 131, 132
Dinosaur Provincial Park, 27, *27*
Dinosaurs, 27, *27*, *76*
Dredge No. 4, 148, *149*
Dulse, 97, *97*

E

Eagles, 26, 147, *147*
Eastern Townships (Que.), 80
Easton, Peter, 117
Edmonton, 28, 29
Ellesmere Island, 140
English language, 68, 82–83
Erie, Lake, 55, 62

F

Falcons, 26
Fathers of Confederation, 86
Festivals, heritage, 45, 49, *50*, 51
Festivals, music, 50, 95, 110
Fiddlehead, 95
Fishing industry, 102, 107, 116
Five Islands, 111

Flags, provincial:
Alberta, 20
British Columbia, 6
Manitoba, 42
New Brunswick, 90
Newfoundland, 112
Nova Scotia, 100
Ontario, 52
PEI, 84
Quebec, 68
Saskatchewan, 32
Flags, territorial:
  Northwest Territories, 126
  Nunavut, 134
  Yukon, 142
Forests, 10–11, *10*, *11*, 34, 95
Forillon National Park, 78, *78*
Forks, the, *46*, 47
Fort Liard (NWT), 132
Fort Qu'Appelle (Sask.), 40
Fortress of Louisbourg (N.S.), 106–107,
  106, *107*
Fort William (Ont.), 54
Fossils, dinosaurs, 27, 29
Francophone identity, 83
Franklin, John, 139
French language, 38, 68, 82–83
Frenchman River, 40
Frobisher Bay, 141
Fundy, Bay of, 94, 96, 102–103, 110
Fur trade, 46, 54, 102

G

Gaelic language, 100
Gagnon, Marcel, *81*
Gaspésie (Gaspé Peninsula), 78–79, *78*,
  79, 92
Georgian Bay (Ont.), 56–57
Gimli (Man.), 45, 49, 50
Glace Bay (N.S.), 108
Glaciers, 14, 15, 28, 119
Glenbow Museum, 28
Glooscap, 111
Gold, panning for, 148
Gold rush, 19, 142, 144, 145, 148,
  149, 151
Gorgosaurus, 27
Grand Manan Island (N.B.), 96–97
Grand Pré (N.S.), 102, *103*
Grasslands National Park, 40
"Graveyard of the Pacific," 10
Great Explosion of 1917, 104
Great horned owl, 26
Great Lakes, 54–55
  (*See also* specific lakes)
Great Rendezvous, 54
Great Sand Hills, 35, *35*
Great Slave Lake, 139
Gros Morne National Park, 118–19
Group of Seven, 57
Guillemots, 109, *109*
Gulf Islands (B.C.), 19

H

Habitat, endangered, 27, 73, 116
Haggis, 110
Halifax, 104
Harrington Harbour (Que.), *77*
Hawks, 26
Head-Smashed-In Buffalo Jump, 24, *24*
Hearne, Samuel, 130
Hidden Lake (NWT), 128
High Arctic, 140
Highland Summer Games (N.S.), 110
Historic Acadian Village, 92–93, *92*
Hockey Hall of Fame, 60, *60*
Hognose snakes, 45
Hoodoos, *28*
Hopewell Cape (N.B.), *98*, 99
Hudson's Bay Company, 46
Humpback whales, 96, *96*, 116
Huron, Lake, 54, 55
Hydroelectric energy, 16

I

Ice ages, 15, 35, 49, 119, 151
Icebergs, 76, 121, *123*
Iceworms, 14
Île Bonaventure (Que.), 78, *79*
Indigo bunting, *66*
Inuit, 31, 134, 137, 138, 139, 141
Inuit art, 141
Inuit language. *See* Inuktitut
Inuksuk, *139*
Inuktitut, 134, *136*, 137, 138
Inuvik (NWT), 133
Invialuktun dialect, 136
Iqaluit, 140
Iqaluktuutiaq (Cambridge Bay), 136–37,
  136, 138–39
Iroquois people, 30, 67, 71
Islendingadagurinn (Man.), 45, *49*, 50

J

James Bay Project, 16
Jasper National Park, 28
Jasper Tramway, 28
Joan of Arc Park, 75

K

Kananaskis Provincial Park, 28
Kejimkujik National Park, 110
Kensington Market (Toronto), 60, *60*
Killarney Provincial Park, 56
Killer whales, *18*
Kingston Buskers Rendezvous, 67
King William Island, 139
Klondike Gold Rush (1898), 142, 144,
  145, 148, 149, 151
Kluane Museum of Natural History, 150
Kluane National Park, 149, *150*
Kouchibouguac National Park, 93, *93*
'Ksan Indian Village, 19

L

Labrador, 114, 120, 121
Lacrosse, *67*
Lac-Saint-Jean (Que.), 80
Lake Superior Provincial Park, 54
La Ronde (Montreal), 81
Leopard frogs, 35
Little Manitou Lake (Sask.), 41
Living Prairie Museum, *51*
Lobsters, 87, *87*, *93*
Lodgepole pines, 34
Logan, Mount, 149, *150*
Long Beach (B.C.), 8, *8*
Louisbourg, siege of (1745), 107
Lynx, 147, *147*

M

Machias Seal Island (N.B.), *99*
Mackenzie, Alexander, 128
Mackenzie River, 126, 139
Magnetic Hill (N.B.), 98, 99
MANITOBA, 42–51
Maritime provinces, 84–123
Matane River (Que.), 81
Mattawa River, 66
Matthew (ship), 117, *117*
Mavillette Beach Provincial Park, 103
Medicine wheel, 39
Men of the Deeps, 108
Métis, 41, 47
Métro (Montreal), 70, *70*
Michigan, Lake, 55
Mi'kmaq people, 30, 88, 93, 111
Milk River (Alta.), 24
Milne, A. A., *51*
Mingan Archipelago National Park, 80
Mining, 108–109
Miramichi folksong festival, 95, 98
Mohawk, 30, *67*
Monarch butterfly, *56*
Montagnais, 77

Montcalm, Louis-Joseph de, 74
Montreal, 70–73
Mont-Royal, 70
Moose, 119, *119*, 147
Moose Jaw, 30, 38
Mosquitoes, 122, 146
Multiculturalism, *50*, 61, 71, 124–25
Musée du Fort, 74
Museum of Civilisation, 65
Museum of Man and Nature, 46
Museum of Science and Technology, 65
Muskoxen, 134, 136, 138, *138*, *140*

Narcisse Wilderness Management Area, 48, 50
Narrows, the (Nfld.), *114*, 115
Native peoples:
    cultural contributions of, 30, *67*
    folklore/traditions, 26, 40, 111
    land claims, 47
    language, 25, 30, 39, 54, 74, 78, 93, 128, 134, *136*, 137, 138
    lifestyle, 31, 39
    powwows, 40, 50
    (*See also* specific groups of)
NEW BRUNSWICK, 90–99
NEWFOUNDLAND
AND LABRADOR, 112–23
New France, 74, 102, 106
Niagara Escarpment, 62
Niagara Falls, 55, 62, *62–63*
Norsemen, 120
North Shore:
    St. Lawrence, 76–77, 82
    Superior, 54, 55
Northern lights, 132
Northern Prairie Skink, 44–45
North-West Mounted Police, 39
Northwest Rebellion (1885), 41, 47, *47*
NORTHWEST TERRITORIES, 126–33
North West Trading Company, 54, *54*
NOVA SCOTIA, 100–111
Nudibranch, 109
NUNAVUT, 134–41

Oak Hammock Marsh, *48*, 49
O Canada, 75
Oil/gas industry, 22, 23
Old Man of the Mountain (Nfld.), 119, *119*
Ogopogo monster, 19
Olympic Stadium (Montreal), 72
ONTARIO, 52–67
Ontario, Lake, 55, 62
Ottawa, 64–65
Ottawa River, 66
Owls, 26

Pacific Coast, 6–19
Parc du Mont-Ste-Anne, 80
Parc de Mont-Tremblant, 80
Parliament Buildings, 58, 64
Peace River, 16
Pelicans, *48*, 49
Petro-Canada building (Calgary), 22
Petroglyphs, 24
Pictographs, 24
Pika, 14
Pingo, 133
Pirates, 117
Pitcher plants, *109*, 112, 119
Plains of Abraham, 74, *74*, 75
Plants, carnivorous, 119
Point Pelee (Ont.), 52
Point Pelee National Park, 66
Pointe-à-Callière Museum of Archeology, 71
Pointe Noire Coastal Station (Que.), 80
Polar Bear Express, 66
Portage and Main streets (Winnipeg), 46

Portage Place (Winnipeg), 46
Portaging, 56
Potato Museum (PEI), 87, 89
Poutine, *80*
Prairie dogs, 36, *36*, 38, 40
Prairie provinces, 20–51
Prairies, the, 20, 36–37, 42
Prince Albert National Park, 40
PRINCE EDWARD ISLAND, 84–89
Prince of Wales Northern Heritage Centre (NWT), 131
Pronghorn antelope, *34*, 35
Province House (PEI), 86, *86*
Puffins, 98, *99*, 116
Pumpjack, 23, *23*

Qiviut, 140
Qu'Appelle Valley, *40*
QUEBEC, 68–81
Quebec City, 74–75
Queen Charlotte Islands, 19
Queen Street West (Toronto), 61

Rainforest, 10–11, 72
Rankin Inlet, 141
Raptors, 26
Rattlesnake, *25*
Red Bay (Lab.), 121
Red River, 47, 49
Red River Rebellion (1869), 47
Red-sided garter snake, 48
Red-tailed hawk, 26
Red-winged blackbird, *48*
Regina, 38–39
Republic of New Iceland, *49*
Revelstoke Dam, 16
Reversing Falls, 94, *94*
Richardson's ground squirrel, 49, *49*
Rideau Canal, 65
Riding Mountain National Park, 50
Riel, Louis, 40, 47, *47*
River Roar Powerboat Races, 41
Rocher Percé (Que.), 78, *79*
Rogers Pass (B.C.), *17*
Royal British Columbia Museum, 19
Royal Canadian Mint, 46, *46*
Royal Canadian Mounted Police (RCMP), *38–39*, 39
Royal Ontario Museum (ROM), 61
Royal Saskatchewan Museum, 38
Royal Winnipeg Ballet, 50

Saguenay River, 80
St. Boniface (Man.), *46*, 47
Saint John (N.B.), 94
Saint John River, 94
Saint John River Valley, 94–95
St. John's (Nfld.), *114–15*
St. John's Harbour, 115
Saint-Laurent (Montreal), 70
St. Lawrence, Gulf of, 76
St. Lawrence River, 74, 76–77, 81
St. Mary's Sea Bird Sanctuary (Nfld.), 122
Sainte-Flavie (Que.), *81*
Salmon, 81
SASKATCHEWAN, 32–41
Saskatchewan Air Show, 41
Saskatoon, 39, 40
Scarlet tanager, *66*
Science North, 57
Scimitar cat, 151
Seagulls, 10
Sea lions, 9, *9*
Seals, 98, *99*
Sea otters, 10
Seasickness, 77
Second World War, 65, 66, 115
Selkirk (Man.), *51*
Service, Robert, *151*
Shediac (N.B.), 93

Shipwrecks, 10, 115, 121
Signal Hill (Nfld.), *114*, 115
Silent Witness Memorial (Nfld.), *117*
Skookum Jim, 149
SkyDome (Toronto), 58
Skytrain, 13, *13*
Snake pits (Narcisse), 48, 50
Snowbirds Gallery, 38
Snow geese, 81
"Sourdoughs," 147
South Nahanni River (NWT), 133
Sparrow hawk, 26
Sparwood (B.C.), 19
Springhill Mining Disaster (1958), 108
Spruce Woods Provincial Park, 44, *44*
Squamish people, 12
S.S. *Klondike*, 145
Standing Buffalo Indian Powwow, 40
Stanley Park, 12
Starvation Cove, 139
Stellar's jay, *18*
Sternwheelers, 145, *145*
Subways, 58, 70
Sudbury (Ont.), 57
Sundews, 119
Sunset Retreat Ceremony, 39, *38–39*
Superior, Lake, 54, 55, *55*

Thelon Game Sanctuary, 140
Thelon River, 140
Thule people, 141
Thunder Bay (Ont.), 54
Tides, 94, *99*, 110
Time zones, 90
Toronto, 58–61
Toronto Blue Jays, 58
Toronto Islands, 59
Tree swallow, *48*
Tuktoyaktuk (NWT), 133, 150
Tundra, 138, 139, 141
Totem poles, *12*
Tulip Festival (Ottawa), 66

Ucluelet (B.C.), 11
Ukrainian Cultural Heritage Village (Alta.), 29
Ukrainian festival (Man.), 50

Vancouver, 12–13
Vancouver Island, 8, *12*
Vegreville (Alta.), 29
Victoria Island, 136
Vikings, 120
Virginia Falls (NWT), *133*
Voyageurs, 34, 54

W.A.C. Bennett Dam, 16
Wanuskewin Heritage Park, 39, *40*, 41
Wascana Centre, 38
Wawa (Ont.), 54
Welland Canal, 62
Welland Centre, *62*
West Edmonton Mall, *29*
Western Development Museum(s), 38, 40
Westray Mine, 108
Whale hunt, 121
Whale watching, *80*, 81, 96–97
Whales: beluga, 73; humpback, 96, *96*, 116, killer, *18*, 19; pilot, *105*
Whitehorse, 145
White Pass & Yukon Route Railway, 144, *144*
White pelican, 49
Winnie the Pooh, *51*
Winnipeg, 46–47, *46*
Winnipeg, Lake, 48, 49, *48–49*
Winnipeg Folk Festival, 50

Winnipeg Symphony Orchestra, 50
Winter carnivals, 67, 81
Winter Olympics (1988), 22
Wolfe, Gen. James, 74
Wolves, 50
Woolly mammoth, 14, 19
Writing-on-Stone Provincial Park, 24

Yellow-headed blackbird, *48*
Yellowknife, 130–31
York-Sunbury Historical Museum, 95
YUKON, THE, 142–151
Yukon River, 142, 145, 146–47
Yukon Sourdough Rendezvous Festival, 150